Web of Light

Web of Light
Rites for Witches in the New Age

MORWYN

A division of Schiffer Publishing Ltd.
77 Lower Valley Road, Atglen, PA 19310

To all members of the Coven of Trer Dryw, past and present, I dedicate this book. Without you it would not have been possible—Blessed Be!

International Standard Book Number: 0-924608-17-X
Library of Congress Catalog Card Number: 93-060949

Cover illustration by Steve Ferguson, Colorado Springs, CO

Published by Whitford Press
A division of Schiffer Publishing Ltd.
77 Lower Valley Road
Atglen, PA 19310
Manufactured in the United States of America
This book may be purchased from the publisher.
Please include $2.95 postage.
Try your bookstore first.

We are interested in hearing from authors
with book ideas on related subjects.

Contents

Preface

Modern-day Wicca, or Witchcraft, as it is commonly known, is a version of an ancient mystery religion filtered through contemporary eyes. Wicca has become the philosophical focus for many people today who feel that their spiritual needs have not been addressed adequately by standard, organized religions. Much confusion and misunderstanding has arisen around the philosophy of Wicca and what Witches do when they worship.

This book comprises the second in a series that treats the subject of Wicca and attempts to divulge some of its mysteries. The first work, *Secrets of a Witch's Coven,* gives a broad basis of understanding of the philosophical tenets of Wicca and leads the seeker on the path to initiation into the first degree of the Craft. It also outlines a brief history of Witchcraft and Magic.

Green Magic, the third volume in the series, discusses the use of herbs, teas, precious stones, and talismans in Magic and healing.

Witch's Brew: A Formulary, the fourth book, describes the importance of fragrance to ritual, and describes how to make and use incenses, perfume oils, potpourris, sachets, ritual baths, and other items in Witchcraft.

The final two books in the series deal with modes of divination and the realm of PSI as it relates to hauntings and apparitions.

This volume, *Web of Light: Rites for Witches in the New Age,* reveals material from my personal Book of Shadows, including rituals and spells used by our coven. If you ever have wondered exactly what Witches do during their rites, this book provides the answers.

The first chapter examines the symbolism of the Circle—the sacred space within which Witches perform all rituals. Why Witches construct Circles before they perform magical operations is explained, and Circle-casting methods are elaborated.

Chapters 2 through 5 offer models for lunar, seasonal, and planetary rituals, as well as rites and spells for specific purposes. Attributes of the planets, Moon phases, and characteristics of the elements are enumerated. The New Moon ritual to understand the element fire includes tips on pyromancy, and the model planetary rite to communicate with animals describes animal symbolism.

The final chapter and the appendix explain the importance of trees in Wicca observances. Ways in which the power radiated by these guardians of our earth can be incorportated into rituals are elaborated, and the properties and magical lore of over forty types of trees are detailed.

The ceremonies delineated in this book have been found to work well for our coven of Trer Dryw. One of the merits of Wicca is that it is a personalized religion, readily adaptable to the specific needs of individuals. In that spirit, I offer these rituals drawn from the soul of our coven. They form a "web of light"—a structure upon which to build individualized rites. It is my sincere hope that you will find them useful.

In Light and Love,
Morwyn

Chapter One
Circle Casting

Circle Symbolism

The Magic Circle of the Adept, the secret space where unimaginable ceremonies shrouded in mystery take place, that sacred center carefully hidden from the eyes of the uninitiated—what *is* a Magic Circle? How does it feel to sit inside a Sacred Circle? How do you make one?

Here I can only describe the Magic Circle and give you instructions on how to construct it. The rest depends on your will and imagination. I can tell you, however, that within a properly formed Magic Circle initiates find a sense of absolute peace, protection, and insulation from the worries of the outside world. It is a place in this world but not of it, one that must be experienced to be believed.

This book forms a compendium of rituals and spells, and the first chapter details the basic steps necessary to any ritual. You will learn to organize and construct a Circle of Light, and to invoke and banish the other worldly energies and entities that help infuse a rite with power.

Before you begin magical operations you need to know how to cast a Circle. You may wonder why Witches, Magicians, and Shamans invariably draw a real or imagined Circle before they invoke spiritual powers. The importance of the Magic Circle becomes evident once you understand Circle symbolism. In *Man,*

Myth and Magic, the circle is cogently defined: "If you want to depict a group of things linked together, complete in itself and separated from everything outside the group, the shape which most effectively expresses completeness and separateness at the same time is the circle." [1]

The circle images the ideas of infinity and eternity, and the perfect wholeness of the divinity. Furthermore, it represents the ultimate state of "at-one-ment" that human beings strive to achieve — especially those of us who follow the gentle path of Wicca. In ancient Greece, this concept was vivified by the symbol of the *ourobouros:* a snake devouring its own tail around which are inscribed the words *En To Pan,* "all is one." The circle also is linked to the perception of zero, or nothingness—the great void out of which all things have the potential to be created.

At the same time the circle stands apart, insulated from outside influences. Once again, the Greeks emphasized this principle with their holy circle dancers who whirled within a circle until they fell into states of ecstasy and felt sensations of displacement or of a standing apart. In such a condition the dancer loses consciousness of self and seeks to identify with the Universe.

Witches cast a Magic Circle to create a sacred space, as in a church, which is insulated from evil, negativity, and other mundane influences. According to Witches and Magicians, the purified sphere constitutes the "right atmosphere" in which to fire the imagination and invoke spiritual forces.

The Magic Circle contains the Witch's powers within it, so that the magical force remains concentrated and channelled directly to the task at hand. For this reason, mediums at seances ask participants to link hands. Similarly, when performing healing rites, Witches raise a cone of power by holding hands in a Circle and chanting or dancing around the person to be healed.

The Sacred Site

You can inscribe a ritual Circle anywhere, but ideally you should set aside a room exclusively for ritual purposes. The room should have a permanent altar and perhaps magic mirrors on each wall as points of focus toward the four cardinal points of the Universe (East, South, West, and North). You even can erect two pillars on either side of the altar and paint one black to represent the forces of the unseen; paint the other white to symbolize manifestation. A permanent sacred site accumulates and retains a vast amount of the power that has been built up by every ritual performed there. Such a place also makes an ideal retreat for meditation or solace for the troubled spirit. Unfortunately, few of us can afford the luxury of a private temple and must therefore keep all ritual accouterments in a portable chest to carry from site to site.

Many Witches also establish a site outdoors, so that they can be closer to the natural currents of the earth, sea, and sky. Suitable locations include atop a hill; deep within a forest; on a lonely shore; in a place that carries an ancient mystical name; or at the point where ley lines (manifestations of earth energies) converge. (Stonehenge in England is perhaps the most famous example of a sacred site built on ley lines. For a complete discussion of ley lines, see Tom Graves's *Needle of Stone Revisited,* Gothic Image Publications, 1986.)

Elements of Circle Casting

The variations for inscribing a Magic Circle are probably as infinite as the circle itself, but Witches of all traditions employ similar general formulas based on common principles. First, the Witch banishes negative and hostile influences from the site and purifies it. Then she invokes other worldly powers to descend and lend their aid to the rite to be performed. Symbols of the elements, including consecrated salt and water, are used in the ceremony, as well as a knife or sword for tracing the confines of the Circle. Names of power are usually spoken, and in one form or another, the Guardians of the Four Quarters of the Universe are invoked.

To close the Circle, the Witch thanks and banishes all spirits and forces that have been attracted to the center of light, for to leave them lurking about invites dissipation of the magical force—and could be downright dangerous.

Other than this basic formula, all else is left open to interpretation based on the beliefs and imagination of the individual.

Traditionally, Witches and Magicians physically draw a nine-foot-diameter Circle and mark it with chalk, cord, dried herbs, flowers, etc. Some practitioners paint or embroider a permanent nine-foot Circle on a piece of cloth, canvas, or carpet that they fold away when not in use. Other Witches simply mark the cardinal points with candles of appropriate colors (yellow for East, red for South, blue for West, green for North). All insist that although the Circle must be physically delineated, the Witch must construct it mentally as well, using such sacred weapons as ritual dagger, sword, ankh—or when all else fails—her extended index and second fingers.

Witches wear simple attire or elaborate robes complete with hood and cordelier (a cord tied around the waist that shows one knot for each degree of initiation), or cast the Circle sky-clad (nude). Some Witches occasionally like to wear street clothes to assure themselves that their efficacy is not tied to physical accouterments such as robes. The only requirement is that Witches should not wear unconsecrated jewelry or anything made from animal products (leather, for example), or shoes, which can interfere with the cosmic energy flow.

Equipment such as dagger, pentacle, lamp, wand, cup, salt celler, sword, cauldron, bell, incense burner, candlesticks, altar cloth, fragrant oils, etc., are all useful ritual items that excite the imagination and draw out the subconscious mind, but they are not necessary. The most experienced Witches and Magicians supposedly are adept enough to devise entire living rituals inside their heads. The rest of us generally prefer to rely on ritual aids to help us expand our consciousnesses.

By painting the symbolic meanings on the elemental weapons, the Witch learns about the nature of the forces they represent. After she consecrates these weapons, they become powerful tools that vibrate with psychic and cosmic energy certainly equal to any magical weapon depicted in fantasy tales. Details about the nature, use, and consecration of ritual equipment are given in my book, *Secrets of a Witch's Coven*.

Guardians of the Quarters

When you cast a Circle you must invoke the powers of the Archangels of the four Quarters of the Universe to protect your Circle from negativity and imbalance, and to infuse your rite with their energy. The Archangels rule the four primary elements out of which all is created: air, fire, water, and earth. The elements and their Guardians are assigned to the cardinal points of the compass—East, South, West, and North. Guardians are sometimes called Watchtowers, Openers of the Gates, or Archangels. They concentrate the pure essence of the elements they represent. Often, in order to visualize such powers, we translate them into humanly-comprehensible terms and envision them as enormous gods robed in the colors of their elements, displaying relevant symbols.

While the Archangels represent concentrations of elemental powers and therefore are neither male nor female, by tradition many Witches and Magicians conceive of them as masculine beings. There is no logical reason for this belief other than acculturation; so if you are more comfortable conceiving of them as female, or androgynous, then this is your prerogative. We call them Guardians because we believe that they protect us, and we endow them with four distinct personalities. The more associations we can muster, the clearer the feeling of the power behind the element and the stronger and truer the image. Descriptions of the Archangels follow.

East: Raphael (Rah-fai-yel)

Archangel of Air and Guardian of the Eastern Quarter of the Universe, Raphael represents the rising Sun and the dawning of inner light upon the psyche. He presides over the mind, speech, communication, and travel. Raphael is the healer god (his name means "god as healer"), and he is the protector of travellers and adventurers. He is a slim, strong figure with gray eyes and brown hair caressed by cool breezes. The wind billows around his yellow, flowing robes as he poises atop a castle or a mountain. He is a winged god, a model of faith and aspiration. In one hand he bears a sword to strike at the heart of all matters, and in the other he carries a caduceus, symbol of his healing abilities.

South: Michael (Mee-Khai-yel)

Archangel of Fire and Guardian of the Southern Quarter of the Universe, the avenging angel and dragonslayer rules the power of light over darkness. He embodies pure, awesome, masculine energy, and sits on the right shoulder of the deity. Ruler of regeneration, Michael also judges souls and cures diseases arising from imbalance. His name means "strong-one of god," and he certainly presents a god-like picture , standing amid a ravaged landscape, clad in armor and saffron robes, holding aloft his power wand. His golden tresses shine in the midday Sun, and his clear blue eyes scintillate in the light.

West: Gabriel (gah-bree-yel)

A gentler being, Gabriel, Ruler of Water and Guardian of the Western Quarter of the Universe, stands in a verdant forest offering in his outstretched hand the chalice of love and compassion. A waterfall tinkles in the background. Gabriel is the bearer of the seed of life, and he represents resurrection, as his name, which means "like unto god," attests. He stands for joy, companionship, and the triumph of life over death. He rules the emotional ebb and flow of all beings as well as the astral plane of existence. This is the angel of the Annunciation as depicted in Christian paintings, who appears as a kind, soft-spoken being with amber-colored eyes, chestnut hair, and light blue raiments.

North: Auriel (Ow-ree-yel) or Uriel (Oo-ree-yel)

The name attributed to this Ruler of Earth and Guardian of the Northern Quarter of the Universe means "enlightenment of god." Auriel represents sustenance, home, the physical body, and the earth mother, giver of life. His robes are an indefinite, dark color, merging into various shades of citrine, olive, russet, gray, and black. His abode is a wheatfield or a cornfield, from where he offers produce of the earth in one hand while holding the shield of the law in the other. Some conceive of him as an elder with black and peppered-gray hair and beard, and wise dark eyes—a being who reads aloud in slow and hushed tones from a weighty tome. However, I see him as a strong, muscular, earthy, vital being with flashing black eyes, flowing dark brown hair, and sensuous lips. To me, he is neither a young nor old man, but one whose knowledge and understanding present a powerful, positive force for earthbound creatures.

Each time you cast and consecrate a Circle you must visualize these Great Lords of the Outer Spaces, for they are your protectors and the channels through which the powers of the elements are transferred to this plane. To invoke these mighty ones, begin in the East and work your way deosil (Sunwise), toward South, West, and North.

Consecration of Salt and Water

Before you invoke the Archangels you will need to learn the fundamental procedure of purification and consecration of salt and water. Salt and water, symbols of the elements earth and water, evoke the substance and life force of the god and goddess principles. When the priestess (or priest) mixes them during the ceremony, she affirms the life-creating powers represented by the combination of these opposite forces. The Witch first banishes negativity from these elements so that they may be pure for the rite; then she consecrates them to the task at hand.

Perform this ritual before opening the temple. First, place the salt and water in dishes (clay for salt, crystal for water) on the altar. Consecrate the elements with your athame or your index and second fingers.

After consecration, you can place the salt and water in the North and West as symbols of the elements. At other times, you may want to leave them on the altar and anoint and bless the other coveners with them. You can also consecrate magical weapons, talismans, stones, and other objects by sprinkling them with these purified and consecrated elements.

After the ritual is over, pour both salt and water on the earth outside (down the drain is permissible if, for example, you live in an apartment complex in the middle of a city). Do not leave the salt and water lying about—doing so shows lack of respect for the elements.

The Rite

To perform the Rite of Consecration of Salt and Water, place the filled bowls on the altar. Light the altar candles (generally, two white candles set at the back of the altar on either side) and empty your mind of daily concerns. As you take your athame in hand, visualize a shaft of brilliant white light descending from the cosmos, entering your body through the top of your head, and exiting from your shoulder, arm, hand, and ritual dagger. As you hold the athame over the bowl of water, call to mind all the forms that water can take, from a still pool to a raging cataract. Feel its wetness permeate your body like a cool, pervasive mist. Say: "Essence of life, fluid of the spirit which courses through all living matter, I exorcise you of negativity and imbalance."

Dip the point of your athame into the water. Recite: "Embodiment of joy and hope for resurrection, be consecrated. By virtue of this sacred blade I transmute you into the blood of the life force."

Extend your athame over the bowl of salt, and contemplate all the forms that earth can take, from lowly grain of sand to Rocky Mountain peaks and valleys. Evoke the smell of damp earth in the fields and feel its warmth and substantiality. Say: "Warm and comforting solidity, in whose womb from our beginnings we were rocked, and to whose darkness we will return, I exorcise you of negativity and imbalance."

Place the point of the athame into the salt, and continue: "You who nourishes our beings and makes us strong, symbol of earth, the only home we know; by virtue of this sacred blade, I transmute you into the body of the divine potency."

Pour some salt into the water and stir clockwise three times with your athame. Repeat: "Herein lies the expression of the mystery of creation."

Rite for Consecration of Cakes and Ale

During some rituals, such as initiation or Sabbats, it is customary to serve cakes and ale as a kind of communion. Coveners partake of specially prepared cookies and honey mead as symbols of the body and blood of the god and goddess, and in this way they incorporate these forces into themselves. The following consecration ritual is easily adaptable to this rite.

Place the mead in a crystal goblet and the cookies (Isis Cakes—see chapter 4 for the recipe) on a pentacle, and perform the rite as you would the rite of consecration of salt and water, up to the point where you mix together the salt and water.

At this juncture, approach each covener, proffer a cake and a sip of wine, and say: "This is the body of the Mountain Mother; this is the blood of the Fertile God. There is no part of you that is not of the god and goddess."

Casting a Circle

Once you learn the rituals outlined above and have consecrated your athame and other ritual tools, you are ready to cast a Circle. If you have not yet acquired a ritual dagger (and they are becoming increasingly expensive and difficult to find), use your index and second fingers as the conduit through which you concentrate your will.

I will describe three procedures for casting and consecrating a Circle. The first is a traditional method employed in Witchcraft; the second is based on principles of Ceremonial Magic. They are both equally effective in most situations, such as Esbats, spells, healing rites, etc. Reserve the third, more complex method for special occasions, such as some Sabbats and initiations: It is not wise to always use the most powerful ritual you know.

Wicca-Way Circle Casting

Measure a nine-foot diameter circle. With a compass, find the exact locations of the cardinal points. Mark them with candles (yellow for East, red for South, blue for West, green for North). Erect an altar in the center of this sacred space facing the East, and cover it with an altar cloth (a plain white tablecloth will suffice). Then place on it candleholders and anointed candles (Temple Rite anointing oil is a good choice for many rituals); flowers, sacred stones, and other offerings; and of course, your ritual tools (dagger, wand, chalice, pentacle).

Light the Quarter candles and altar candles, and consecrate the salt and water. Place an incense burner with a quick-lighting coal and Witches' Circle incense in the East, consecrated water in the West, and consecrated salt or loam in the North. Some Witches place a crystal in the North in addition to the salt. The red Quarter candle in the South stands for fire.

Leave the readied Circle and go to your bathroom to soak in a tub of warm water to which you have added rose oil with a sprig of rosemary. Dress appropriately (robed or skyclad—no leather, fur, or unconsecrated jewelry) and return to the Circle.

Beginning in the East, light the incense, lift the burner aloft toward the outside of the Circle, and call aloud: "Spirit of Air, enter into this the symbol of your element, and banish negativity and imbalance from the sacred site."

Slowly move around the perimeter, swinging the incense burner to purify the Circle. As in all rituals, move deosil; that is, with the Sun, from East to South, West, and North, and back to the East again. Moving in the opposite direction (called "widdershins") is only used in rituals of destruction when you wish to invoke some rather nasty demonic spirits. In Wicca, we never move widdershins while in the Circle, even when picking up objects, visiting the altar, dancing, etc. Contrary movements confuse the magical force.

Once you return to the East with the incense burner, raise it in both hands, and silently thank the spirits of Air for entering into the element.

Move to the South, take up the candle, and again in your own words thank the spirits of Fire for entering into the element. Carry the candle around the Circle, as you did with the incense burner, ending in the South. Hold it aloft, and give silent thanks.

Beginning in the West, thank the spirits of Water, and sprinkle the water as you walk to mark the Circle. Repeat the procedure in the North with salt, thanking the spirits of Earth.

Take your athame from the altar, and holding it pointed upwards, return to the East. Stand with your feet spread apart slightly, arms open and raised at your shoulders, and invoke: "Raphael, healer and teacher of humankind, you who awakens us to our inner life, I call upon you to descend into this Circle of Light to protect us from evil and to lend us your power so we can work the will of the Lord and Lady."

Point your athame horizontally at shoulder level and trace in the air the Quadrant of the Circle from East to South. Visualize a flaming bluish-white light emitting from your athame and forming the Quadrant of the Circle.

Take the same posture in the South as you did in the East. Remember to invoke with conviction and authority: "Michael, Strong-One of god, you who harmonizes the forces of the Universe and triumphs over wrong with your right, you who brings us into balance, I call upon you to descend into this Circle of Light to protect us from evil and to lend us your power so we can work the will of the Lord and Lady!"

Continue tracing the brilliant ring with your athame. Endeavor to keep building the Circle of Light. The vision of this pulsating ring of light should never leave you as you invoke. In the West intone: "Gabriel, potency of god, bearer of the chalice of love, from whom we receive the divine spark, I call upon you to descend into this Circle of Light to protect us from evil and lend us your power so we can work the will of the Lord and Lady!"

Carry the point of light to the North, imagining, as you have with the other Archangels, Auriel in all his splendor. Say: "Auriel, light of god, bringer of knowledge, truth and divine love, you who instills us with awe for the wonders of creation, I call upon you to descend into this Circle of Light to protect us from evil and to lend us your power so we can work the will of the Lord and Lady!"

Finish inscribing the Circle of Light, ending in the East. Imagine that it now flames around you like a ring of fire. Go to the northeast Quadrant of the Circle, stand with one hand pointing toward the heavens and the other, holding your athame, pointed toward the ground, and pronounce: "By virtue of this sacred blade I hereby declare this Circle purified, consecrated, and open to the spirits! We are at one with the god and goddess."

At last you are ready to work Magic.

When it is time to draw the ritual to a close, stand in the East as you did when you opened the Circle, and declare: "Raphael, god as healer, I thank you for enveloping us in your protective mantle. Depart now to your airy realm and remain there in perfect love and perfect peace, until once again you deem to grace our Circle of Light with your presence. Blessed Be!"

In the South, call: "Michael, god as strength, I thank you for enveloping us in your protective mantle. Depart now to your fiery realm and remain there in perfect love and perfect peace until once again you deem to grace our Circle of

Light with your presence. Blessed Be!"

In the West, intone: "Gabriel, image of god, I thank you for enveloping us in your protective mantle. Depart now to your watery realm and remain there in perfect love and perfect peace until once again you deem to grace our Circle of Light with your presence. Blessed Be!"

In the North, speak: "Auriel, god as enlightenment, I thank you for enveloping us in your protective mantle. Depart now to your earthly realm and remain there in perfect love and perfect peace until once again you deem to grace our Circle of Light with your presence. Blessed Be!"

Return to the East, and with legs apart and arms outstretched toward the heavens, pronounce: "We are grateful for the presence of all entities who have been attracted to our center of power. Now I bid you license to depart to your other worlds in perfect love and perfect peace. The rite is ended. *I A O* (Ee—Aah—Ohh)."

Never forget to banish the spirits who have attended your rite. It is not fair to them to keep them around when you are through using their powers. In fact, if you do not properly banish them, it is possible that their force may be diluted. They also may begin to play tricks on you, or perhaps they may choose never again to appear before you.

Rather than visualizing the Guardians of the Quarters as male beings, some Witches see them as Amazonic female entities. Others balk at what they consider a Judeo-Christian conception of the Guardians as angelic beings. Such Witches may invoke the Guardians as pure, raw energies. However you choose to visualize and summon these representations of the four elements is up to you. No single right way exists. What matters is that you create in your mind an irrefutably clear picture of these powers so that you may harness their energies toward magical workings. As you steadily continue to perform exercises and meditations to direct your imagination, you will find these energies increasingly easier to muster.

Lesser Banishing and Invoking Pentagram Rituals

The second way to open the Circle is via the Lesser Banishing and Invoking

Pentagram rituals, which originate in Ceremonial Magic. It is not within the confines of this book to dwell at length on the esoteric significance of these rituals. If you wish to learn more about the pentagram rituals I suggest that you read my book, *Secrets of a Witch's Coven;* Israel Regardie's *Ceremonial Magic* (Aquarian Press, 1980); or William Gray's *Inner Traditions of Magic* (Weiser, 1984). Nonetheless, on the basis of the summarized information I present here, you can create a potent ritual.

The Lesser Banishing and Invoking Pentagram rituals are so named because they are employed in routine Magic. The Greater Pentagram rituals that follow are reserved for special occasions. All three of these rituals are preceded by another ritual called the Qabalistic Cross.

QABALISTIC CROSS RITUAL

The prelude to the Pentagram rituals is the Qabalistic Cross Ritual. Always begin and end each segment of both the Lesser and Greater Pentagram Rituals with the Qabalistic Cross. This rite centers your energy and affirms that you are about to leave the mundane for the spiritual world of Magic.

The ritual resembles the manner in which Catholics cross themselves. Stand facing East, with feet comfortably apart, and hold your athame pointed upward in your hand. As you pronounce the god names, imagine that a ray of brilliant white light from above penetrates your body, first from head to toe, and then from right to left shoulder. The rays scintillate as you intone. When you finish the ritual, these rays of light should extend outward from your body into infinity. Vibrate the words of power forcefully so that you feel the energy pulsate through your entire body.

The rite is summarized as follows. Say:

"Ateh" (thou, to thee). Touch your third eye.

"Malkuth" (kingdom). Touch your solar plexus, extending the shaft of light to your feet.

"ve-Geburah" (and severity, justice, power). Touch your right shoulder.

"ve-Gedulah" (and the glory, judgment, magnificence). Touch your left shoulder.

"le Olahm Amen" (throughout eons and eons, so mote it be). Clasp your

hands together over your chest.

Now that you know how to perform the Qabalistic Cross Ritual, you can open your Circle using the Lesser Banishing and Invoking Pentagram Rituals. These two rituals are exactly alike, except that when you perform the Banishing Ritual you trace banishing Earth pentagrams, and for the Invoking Ritual you draw invoking Fire pentagrams. The advantage of these rituals over the Wicca Way for opening a Circle is that they can stand alone without recourse to Quarter candles, symbols of the elements, etc. You can perform them any-where, even silently in your head. You can rely on the Banishing Ritual by itself whenever you feel you are undergoing acute stress. For example, I do it silently every time I board an airplane.

To open the Circle, perform the Qabalistic Cross Ritual, the Banishing Ritual, the Qabalistic Cross again, the Invoking Ritual, and finish with the Qabalistic Cross. Execute these rituals with your athame, beginning in the East and moving deosil around the Circle as you do for the Wicca Circle-casting method. Draw down the same shaft of electric bluish-white light to encircle the

Banishing Pentagram of Earth   *Invoking Pentagram of Fire*

Figure 1: The Lesser Banishing and Invoking Pentagrams

sacred space. At the Quarters, cause this ray to swell to the shape of a radiant pentagram, which you then hurl out into space. The pentagram is a powerful symbol in Witchcraft and Magic. It represents the operator's command over the elements and the desire to develop spiritually.

When you draw the pentagrams with your athame, begin at your left hip, moving upwards for banishing, and at your right shoulder, moving downward, for invoking (figure 1).

The ritual follows.

LESSER BANISHING AND INVOKING PENTAGRAM RITUAL

I. Stand facing the East and perform the Qabalistic Cross
II. Perform the Lesser Banishing Pentagram Ritual by drawing Banishing Earth
   Pentagrams
   A. In the East say, *"Yod Heh Vau Heh"* (self-existent one)
   B. In the South say, *"Adonai"* (lord)
   C. In the West say, *"Eheyeh"* (one self)
   D. In the North say, *"Ateh Gebur le-Olahm Adonai"* (thou art the
      power throughout the ages and ages)
III. Return to the East and finish inscribing the Circle. Call to the Archangels
   of the Quarters:
   "Before me, Raphael!
   Behind me, Gabriel!
   To my right, Michael!
   To my left, Auriel!
   Around me flame the pentagrams,
   Above me shines the six-rayed star!"
IV. Perform the Qabalistic Cross
V. Perform the Lesser Invoking Pentagram Ritual, repeating the above invo-
   cation, using Invoking Fire Pentagrams
VI. Return to the East and perform the Qabalistic Cross

Now pause for a moment and experience the awe of the immense power you have harnessed swirling around you. Then go to the northeast Quadrant of the Circle and take the stance of the Magician figure in the tarot (facing inward, one arm raised, fingers reaching to the heavens, the other arm lowered, athame in hand pointed down to the ground).

Declare: *"Hekos, hekos, este bebeloi!* I hereby declare this Circle open."

To close the Circle, perform the Qabalistic Cross in the East, the Banishing Ritual, and Qabalistic Cross (again, in the East). Thank the elementals, spirits, fairies, and unseen guests who have attended your Circle of Light, and send them back to whence they came in the power of *YHVH* (Yod He Vau He). The rite is over.

The Greater Pentagram Ritual

Besides its advanced degree of complexity, what distinguishes the Greater Pentagram Ritual from the Lesser is that you will employ the Greater less frequently; that is, only on important occasions, such as the eight Sabbats, initiations, or when strong protective or invocational powers are required, as in rituals of uncrossing and psychic self-defense. These rituals are also called the Flaming Pentagram Rituals. They are named for the ray of light that issues from each angle of the Pentagram and which reaffirms the forces of the divine light inherent in the pentagram's form. When performing the ritual, envision this flame.

The Greater Pentagram Rituals are indeed eclectic in that they use Hebrew names of power popularized by eighteenth-century Magicians; Egyptian posturing extracted from the writings of the Hermetic Order of the Golden Dawn; Enochian calls (an angelic language developed by Dr. John Dee in Elizabethan times); and representations of the signs of the zodiac. The pronunciation given here for the Enochian calls is what is in vogue at this time. However, at the one-hundred-year anniversary of the founding of the Golden Dawn conference, which I attended in London in 1987, scholars cast doubt on the current pronunciation custom and offered a more Elizabethan rendition. More research needs to be done concerning proper pronunciation procedures. In the meantime, I pass on to you what I learned. You need not understand all

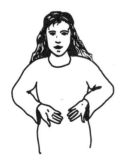

Posture 5=6: The Rending of the Veil

Posture 3=8: The Sign of Practicus

Posture 2=9: The Sign of Theoricus

Posture 1=10: The Sign of Zelator

Posture 4=7: The Sign of Philosophus

The Closing of the Veil

Figure 2: Postures for the Greater Pentagram Ritual

the meanings of these symbols at this time; you will find the ritual effective in any case. If you are curious to read further, I recommend Israel Regardie's weighty volume, *The Golden Dawn* (Llewelyn Publications, 1978) and Dee's lengthy treatise, *The Enochian Evocation of Dr. John Dee* (edited and translated by Geoffrey James, Heptangle Books, 1984).

When performing the Greater Pentagram Rituals, begin by banishing with the Lesser Banishing Ritual, which you have already learned. (You may also use the Greater Banishing Ritual, which forms the Pentagrams in reverse from the formations used in the Greater Invoking Pentagram Ritual.) Remember to initiate and end each major segment of the ritual (banishing, invoking, banishing) with the Qabalistic Cross.

As with other ceremonial workings you have learned, intone the names of power fully and deeply. Trace the Pentagrams with your athame or wand, conjuring all the while a continuous flow of blue-white light emanating from your weapon. Never terminate the flow of energy until after you have completed the ritual.

The postures you assume during the ritual (figure 2) are those taken by initiates to various degrees of the Golden Dawn and other Hermetic orders. These degrees are called Zelator, Theoricus, Practicus, and Philosophus. The numbers associated with them refer to these degrees.

Another posture, the Rending of the Veil that separates mortals from higher knowledge, also comes into play when invoking. When banishing, perform the gesture in reverse to show the Closing of the Veil. Regardie in *The Golden Dawn* describes the signs of the zodiac and the other symbols as follows:

Air hath a watery symbol, because it is the container of rain and moisture. Fire hath the form of the Lion-Serpent. Water hath the alchemic Eagle of distillation. Earth hath the laborious (Ox). Spirit is produced by the One operating in all things. [2]

The circle or Wheel answereth to the all-pervading Spirit: The laborious Ox is the symbol of Earth; the Lion is the vehemence of Fire; the Eagle, the Water flying aloft as with wings when she is vaporized by the force of heat; the Man is the Air, subtle and thoughtful, penetrating hidden things. [3]

THE RITUAL

With this background in mind, you are ready to begin. Face East; perform the Qabalistic Cross. Make the Equilibrated Active Pentagram of Spirit (figure 3). Intone *EXARP* (Ex-ar-pay) after you draw the Pentagram. Make the Spirit Wheel in the center of the Pentagram and say *EHEIEH* (Eh-hay-yeh). Make the 5=6 Rending of the Veil gesture. Formulate the Invoking Pentagram of Air, while intoning *ORO IBAH*

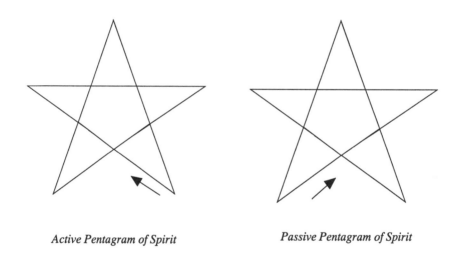

Active Pentagram of Spirit   *Passive Pentagram of Spirit*

Figure 3: Equilibrated Pentagrams of Spirit

AOZPI (Or-oh Ee-ba-hay Ah-oh-zod-pee). Draw the Sigil of Aquarius in the center of the pentagram and say, *YOD HEH VAU HEH* (Yod Hay Vau Hay). Finish with the 2=9 gesture.

Keeping your arm outstretched and without breaking the flow of blue-white light, move to the South. Here trace the Equilibrated Active

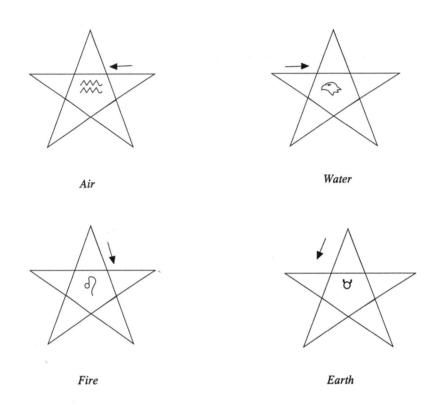

Figure 4: Greater Invoking Pentagrams

Pentagram of Spirit and Greater Invoking Pentagram of Fire (figure 4).

In the West begin with the Equilibrated Passive Pentagram of Spirit, and end with the Pentagram of Water.

In the North, again describe an Equilibrated Passive Pentagram of Spirit, and follow with the Pentagram of Earth.

Lastly, move from North to East to complete the Circle and invoke the Archangels of the Quarters, as you do in the Lesser Pentagram Ritual. Likewise, finish with the Qabalistic Cross.

If properly executed, this is a most satisfying and potent ritual.

THE GREATER PENTAGRAM RITUAL (INVOKING)

I. East

    A. Equilibrated Active Pentagram of Spirit

        EXARP (Ex-ar-pay)

        Wheel of Spirit

        EHEIEH (Eh-hay-yeh)

        5=6 posture

    B. Pentagram of Air (invoking)

        ORO IBAH AOZODPI (Or-oh Ee-bah-hay Ah-oh-zod-pee)

        Air Sigil

        YOD HEH VAU HE (Yod Hay Vau Hay)

        2=9 posture

II. South

    A. Equilibrated Active Pentagram of Spirit

        BITOM (bee-toe-em)

        Wheel of Spirit

        5=6 posture

    B. Pentagram of Fire (invoking)

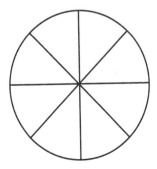

Figure 5: The Wheel of Spirit

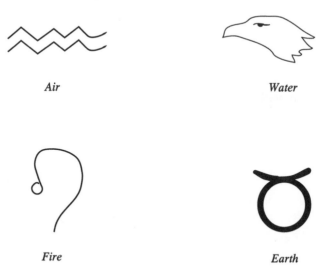

Figure 6: Air, Fire, Water, and Earth Sigils for the Greater Pentagram Ritual

OIP TEAA PEDOCE (Oh-ee-pay Tay-ah-ah Pay-doh-kay)
Fire Sigil
4=7 posture

III. West
    A. Equilibrated Passive Pentagram of Spirit
        HCOMA (Hay-co-em-mah)
        Wheel of Spirit
        ATEH GEBUR LE OLHAM ADONAI (Ah-tah Geh-boor lay
        Oh-lahm Ah-doh-nye)
        5=6 posture
    B. Pentagram of Water (invoking)
        EMPEH ARSEL GAIOL (Em-pay-hay Ar-es-el Gah-ee-ol)
        Water Sigil

AL (Ahl)

3=8 posture

IV. North

    A. Equilibrated Passive Pentagram of Spirit

        NANTA (En-ah-en-tah)

        Wheel of Spirit

        5=6 posture

    B. Pentagram of Earth (invoking)

        EMOR DIAL HECTEGA (Emor Dee-al Hay-cah-tay-gah)

        Earth Sigil

        ADONAI (Ah-doh-nye)

        1=10 posture

V. Return to the East. Call upon Archangels of the Quarters

VI. Qabalistic Cross

THE GREATER PENTAGRAM RITUAL (BANISHING)

I. East

    A. Closing Active Pentagram of Spirit

        EXARP (Ex-ar-pay)

        Wheel of Spirit

        EHEIEH (Eh-hay-yeh)

        Close the Veil

    B. Pentagram of Air (banishing)

        ORO IBAH AOZODPI (Or-oh Ee-bah-hay Ah-oh-zod-pee)

        Air Sigil

        YOD HEH VAU HE (Yod Hay Vau Hay)

        2=9 posture

II. South

A. Closing Active Pentagram of Spirit

BITOM (bee-toe-em)

Wheel of Spirit

Close the Veil

B. Pentagram of Fire (banishing)

OIP TEAA PEDOCE (Oh-ee-pay Tay-ah-ah Pay-doh-kay)

Fire Sigil

4=7 posture

III. West

A. Closing Passive Pentagram of Spirit

HCOMA (Hay-co-em-mah)

Wheel of Spirit

ATEH GEBUR LE OLHAM ADONAI (Ah-tah Geh-boor lay
Oh-lahm Ah-doh-nye)

Close the Veil

B. Pentagram of Water (banishing)

EMPEH ARSEL GAIOL (Em-pay-hay Ar-es-el Gah-ee-ol)

Water Sigil

AL (Ahl)

3=8 posture

IV. North

A. Closing Passive Pentagram of Spirit

NANTA (En-ah-en-tah)

Wheel of Spirit

Close the Veil

B. Pentagram of Earth (banishing)

EMOR DIAL HECTEGA (Emor Dee-al Hay-cah-tay-gah)

Earth Sigil

ADONAI (Ah-doh-nye)

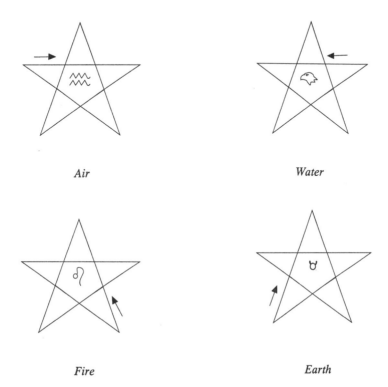

Air

Water

Fire

Earth

Figure 7: Greater Banishing Pentagrams

1=10 posture

V. Return to the East. Call upon Archangels of the Quarters

VI. Qabalistic Cross

Music in Ritual

No one will deny the power of music to stimulate our intellects and emotions. As such, it has figured prominently in ritual for centuries. Not all rituals need music; indeed, none requires it. Nevertheless, music energizes the Circle because it reaches the inner depths of our subconscious minds and allows us to work Magic effectively. Music speaks to us in ways words cannot; it stimulates our emotions, like a painting. It communicates an experience rich in multi-layered levels of meaning.

Also, music creates a pleasant and relaxing atmosphere; it is an especially good way to break the ice in Circles where people not previously acquainted are brought together. In Circle, singing is a great communal activity that fosters joviality and fellowship. Music is an ideal way to teach Pagan children about the lessons of Wicca because it circumvents the necessity for intellectual understanding. Think of all the nursery rhymes and songs you remember from childhood effortlessly because music taught you in a subliminal way!

Finally, musical vibrations and rhythms pulsate with the cosmic rhythm of life. The sound waves beat in synchronization with certain cosmic energies and draw power to the rite.

Some theorists attribute even more far-reaching influences to the effects of sound and music. One of these theorists, Cyril Scott, put forth his ideas in a book entitled *Music: Its Secret Influence Throughout the Ages.*[4] He first published the work in 1933 and updated it in 1958. Due to renewed interest in the subject, the book has undergone several reprints (1973, 1976, 1982). Because Scott's ideas seem to have influenced some writers involved in New Age pursuits such as Wicca, I wish to express my opinions on his work.

Scott argues that both emotional content of music and musical form itself are reproduced in human conduct, and further, that music affects the mind and emotions, both consciously and unconsciously, by means of direct and indirect suggestion and reiteration. To bolster his theory, he cites historical sources such as the ancient East Indian Vedic scriptures, which purport that the entire cosmos was created by sound. He also quotes such giants of Western philosophy as Plato and Aristotle, who posited that music molds character and that any new kind of music runs the danger of imperiling the political institutions of the day. Such notions are not dissimilar to those espoused by certain conservative Christian sects today.

Scott discusses how the *devas* (nature spirits, elementals, angels and Archangels who reside on other planes) transmit their knowledge to humanity through music. Supposedly these entities choose music as a medium because it is the only way they can contact human beings, who otherwise may not be able to perceive them. According to Scott, music affects the senses, emotions, intellect, and spirit. Moreover, Scott alleges that the *devas* have chosen certain human vehicles; i.e., composers, to impart information to the human race as they think we are ready to apprehend it. Even if people do not listen to or hear music, Scott insists, they are affected by it, because the sound waves spread out in concentric circles and are assimilated by the aura, if not by the ear.

He details forms of music prevalent in major cultures throughout history and underscores works of various composers whom, he avows, have been *deva*-directed.

Frankly, I do not subscribe to many of Scott's tenets. In the first place, I simply do not believe that spirits exist who constantly attempt to inform and direct us by these means. Although I do not deny the existence of elementals, angels, Archangels, etc., I do not think that these spirits are bent on bettering the human race.

Secondly, I believe that to attribute to music, and to music alone, the rise and fall of great civilizations is utter nonsense. I agree that music reflects, and to some extent influences culture, particularly in recent times. As musicians, composers, and other artists realized their powers to influence others, they broke away from the domination of the Church (religion) and government and became more free to express their own world visions.

An example of this kind of influence is the Modernist movement of the 1920's in Brazil, during which composers, along with other artists, created a new vision of the future for Brazilians to live by. Another illustration is found in the effects of jazz on American culture. Jazz spread the message of one socio-economic group to a variety of people who, were it not for this musical form and its proponents, would never even have come in contact with this element of society, let alone felt empathy for the people and situations expressed in jazz themes. But the notion that the fates of nations are sealed by the commands of extra-terrestrial beings strikes me as ludicrously fatalistic.

Unfortunately, this high silliness also commits a greater sin: it ignores the personal creativity of the composer, and by analogy, the creativity of all artists, and converts them into mouthpieces of some so-called higher intelligence. In speaking of the plastic arts (which applies equally to music), Andre Malraux wrote about the nature of creativity in *The Voices of Silence* (Doubleday, 1953). Malraux argues that artists have always had the urge to create, which he calls a "will-to-art." This desire has led artists to attempt to make sense of and dominate a Universe over which they previously felt that they had exerted little control. Artists, although admittedly influenced by their own cultures and times as well as by higher powers, are individualistic with regard to their interpretations and expressions.

Joseph Frank, a well-known literary critic, expresses this point of view about creative capabilities when he states in his book, *The Widening Gyre,* that the artist, particularly the modern artist, is not necessarily subject to the dictates of society or culture:

> So far as he is a creator, the artist does not belong to a collectivity that merely sustains a culture but to one which develops it, whether he cares about doing so or not. His creative faculty does not submit him to a fatality become intelligible; it links him to the millennial creative power of man, to cities rebuilt from the ruins, to the discovery of fire. [5]

> The fanatical and often heroic dedication of the modern artist to his mission reveals that he has by no means abandoned his age-old status as a transmitter of the highest spiritual values. Now, however, these values are not derived from the "gods" of his culture; they stem exclusively from his own activity as an artist, from his religious devotion to the function of art itself as the source of a new realm of "the sacred". [6]

Nor are artists subject to the whims of the *devas.* Their inspiration may be sparked by the divine, but it is the spark of divinity within the artists or composers themselves from which their creative images emerge.

Regardless of music's origin, its sway over peoples' emotions and intellect is undeniable. However, it is wrong to assume that music so influences entire civilizations as to bring about their rise and fall. Equally fallacious is to conclude that *devas* direct the process and outcome of rituals, despite the Witch's input. Music may aid the Witch by enhancing visualization. It may even inspire the ritual to great emotional heights, but the Witch remains undeniably in control of the operation. One can view Witches as artists who create their own reality through ritual. They too, use their own creative powers to build images on this plane, which they then set into action. In the same vein I do not believe that major Western composers were unconsciously directed by *devas*—inspired at times by higher powers, perhaps, but never manipulated!

The music of Bach, for example, profoundly affects the intellect. Bach's *Passion of St. Matthew,* a harmonizing and dedicatory work, is perfect for playing at the Fall Equinox. Its image of the father god who showers humanity with divine love encourages one to look forward to the new spiritual year ahead.

Beethoven, on the other hand, expresses the spectrum of experience of the human emotions by way of sound. His music elicits memories in which the content of the subconscious mind is revealed.

Refer to the Sabbat Planner at the end of chapter 4 for other suggestions for using music in ritual.

Relationship of Dance to Ritual

These days, dance often is excluded from rituals This is unfortunate, because dance can exert a powerful influence over rites. Since Paleolithic times, dance has been understood as an important mode for spiritual expression. It provides a universal outlet for the free expression of emotions. Dance also symbolizes the act of creation. Through dance it is possible to find true "at-one-ment," or unity with the divine principle. Long has it been believed that dance contains its own inherent powers. As Roderyk Lange explains in *The Nature of Dance,* behind this power lies the "belief that actions and words technically unrelated to a phenomenon can exert upon it a physical effect." [7]

At one time or another, all cultures have incorporated dancing into their spiritual activities. For instance, heel prints dug into the earth in front of Paleolithic drawings of dancers found on cave walls show that the notion of dancing in worship is ancient indeed. In Japanese Shinto dancing, another ancient tradition, the dancer is believed to be empowered to contact the gods and transmit messages of solace to and from deceased ancestors. From ancient Greece hail the frenzied rites of Dionysus, which are infamous even today.

The Judeo-Christian heritage also has relied upon dancing to lend power to rites. For example, dances are still performed at Hannukah. In the early days of the Roman Catholic Church the faithful danced at funerals of martyrs and at holidays to honor the Virgin Mary. Although the association of dance with Paganism eventually led the Church to suppress dancing, the interdict did not succeed entirely. Today religious dancing is still practiced in parts of Spain and Latin America to celebrate various festivals. For example, the Catholic Church in Brazil finally yielded to the populace's demands and permits dancing in processionals and parades. Pagan cults in Africa and Brazil traditionally rely on dancing to achieve a state of trance in order for participants to become possessed by spirits.

Pagans dance for many reasons. Dancing to achieve a trance state wherein the dancer finds unity with the cosmic forces can be one goal, and dancing usually takes place at the Sabbats to celebrate the seasonal turn of the Wheel of Life. By dancing, the coven comes together in fellowship, focuses energy, and perhaps penetrates the veil of the worlds beyond. It is an ancient belief that dancing bestows fertility on people, animals, and crops. When we leap the cauldron, we imitate the growth of crops, expansion of the mind, and personal creativity.

Among types of dances commonly performed by covens are:

Circle dances. These are round dances performed around a person (to be healed, etc.) or an object (cauldron, bonfire, picture, etc.) in order to raise a cone of power or to develop rapport among coveners. The object in the center of the Circle focuses the group's energy.

Carol. This round dance is accompanied by singing, usually in praise of the god, goddess, or Child of Promise.

Processional. This dance provides a convenient and ceremonial way to enter or leave the ritual space. During the dance, coveners carry candles and pass by the altar where they are anointed with fragrant oils in purification and blessing.

Spiral. An imitation of the "dance of life," it is usually led by the Priest or Priestess. As the dancers enter a progressively complex twisting and intertwining pattern, they symbolically penetrate the maze of the sacred mysteries.

Line. Line dances are performed with couples who face each other. The couples represent the interplay of the positive and negative forces that propel the Universe.

A bumper sticker I saw recently proclaims, "Dance is a lift." It is an exhilarating, powerful experience fraught with inner meaning and an inspiration for rituals over centuries. I urge you to experiment with dance by incorporating its energizing excitement into your rituals.

You are now equipped with the essential tools for working Circle magic. You can erect a circle and open and close it by using the proper equipment, and you know something of the philosophy behind the circle and Circle Casting. In the following chapters you will see how these principles are put into effect.

Chapter Two
Esbat Rites

To the Moon
Greeting to you, gem of the night!
Beauty of the skies, gem of the night!
Mother of the stars, gem of the night!
Foster-child of the sun, gem of the night!
Majesty of the stars, gem of the night! [8]

People from cultures across time and space have experienced the seductive enchantment of the Moon. Fascinating lore about the Moon's power abounds in the oral and written traditions of most societies. And as a grain of truth exists in most myths, so the Moon had been proven to influence our lives.

Science tells us that the Moon affects the gravitational field, weather, tides, fertility, plant growth, and human and animal physical and psychological behavior. As Witches, we strive to attune ourselves to the rhythmic movements of the Universe. We accept the ebb and flow of the Moon in our lives and strive to live in harmony with its magnetic force.

In so doing, we behave no differently from our ancestors. They lived by the thirteen-month lunar calendar and evolved names and attributes for each full Moon of the year that corresponded to the natural phenomena of their environment. They even associated god and goddess forms with the Moon in order describe the characteristics of each season.

I wish to share with you the lunar wisdom developed by American Indians, goddess-worshippers, and the ancient Anglo-Saxons. When you write your own rituals, these peoples' thoughts about the Moon may help to inspire you.

Moon Names

American Indian

The American Indians' vision of the Moon reflects their closeness to nature and dependence on the lunar cycles to forecast when to plant, harvest, hunt animals, etc. These concerns are expressed in their names for each month.

January	Wolf or Old Moon—the famished wolf prowls and howls around the door
February	Snow or Hunger Moon—as hunting becomes more difficult in the heavy snows, famine spreads among the tribes
March	Worm, Crow, Crust or Sap Moon—the ground softens enough for worm castings to appear, and the alternate freezing and thawing creates a crusty snow; time to tap the maple for its sugar
April	Pink, Sprouting Grass, Egg or Fish Moon—pink phlox blooms and sprouting grass harbingers spring; eggs fill birds' nests; fish migrate upstream to spawn
May	Full Flower, Corn, Planting or Milk Moon—newborns suckle and flowers carpet the woods and meadows
June	Strawberry or Rose Moon—the succulent fruit bears prolifically and the air fills with the sweet scent of the blooming rose
July	Buck or Thunder Moon—antlers appear on young bucks, and terrible thunderstorms rage

August	Sturgeon or Red Moon—sturgeons are easily caught; the Moon rises red through the sultry atmosphere
September	Harvest Moon—the bounty of Mother Earth is collected and stored
October	Hunter Moon—time to seek the fattened deer
November	Beaver Moon—set traps for beavers now
December	Cold or Long Nights Moon—winter fastens its icy grip and the days are shortest

Goddess/Feminist Moons

Goddess-oriented religions often conceive of the Moon in a more symbolic, ethereal way than other traditions. This is shown by the divine names they chose for each lunation.

January	Bertha or Earth Mother Moon—birth
February	Brigit or Aphrodite Moon—awakening
March	Rhiannon or Ishtar Moon—passion
April	Cordelia or Luna Moon—visions
May	Branwen or Cybele Moon—magic
June	Morgan le Fey or Mabh Moon—fairies
July	Isis or Danu Moon—thunder
August	Diana or Freya Moon—wisdom
September	Venus or Anu Moon—harvest
October	Hathor Moon—trance
November	Hecate Moon—hunt
December	Nut Moon—oak

Anglo-Saxon Moons

Although the Anglo-Saxon names parallel the Indian names in some respects, the milder climate of Britain is reflected in their names. Also, the particular activities of which the ancient Anglo-Saxons partook at different seasons are commemorated. These activities included distilling mead, gathering herbs, harvesting barley, and making blood sacrifices so that the coming year would be fruitful.

January	Aefter Yule Moon or Wulf Moon—season of the wolf
February	Mire Moon—season of freezing snows
March	Hraed or Hlyd Moon—season of rugged storms
April	Eastre Moon—season of rebirth and chastity
May	Preo-Meolc Moon—season of the seed and three-milkings
June	Sear Moon—season of the hare and mild weather
July	Maed Moon—season of mead and meadow
August	Wyrt or Wort Moon—season of the herb
September	Gust Moon—season of barley; holy season
October	Wyn Moon—season of wine, wind, and storm-felling
November	Blot Moon—season of blood and sacrifice
December	Yule Moon—season of the wheel of the year and the return of the Sun

Moon Phases

Although the lunar names have particular associations with the subtle seasonal changes, the following divisions by Moon phase are even more important. This is because the Moon exerts different types of influences in each phase, depending on whether it is new, waxing, full, or waning. It is wise to plan rituals accordingly. Use this chart as a reference.

New Moon	New beginnings. Make plans, start afresh, begin new projects, gather seeds.
Waxing Moon	Construction. Execute creative, constructive rituals,

	plant most crops, graft and prune trees.
Full Moon	Completion. Perform constructive rituals which require a dose of power or a special push; complete rituals begun during the waxing Moon; execute rituals of wish fulfillment, love, attracting money, and some health spells; harvest crops; babies are easier to birth at this time.
Waning Moon	Draw within. Enact rituals for crossing, uncrossing, protection, exorcism, and psychic self-defense; a time to draw into yourself, to analyze and meditate on what occurred during the waxing Moon; study the direction in which to proceed; rest and renew your energies; undertake clairvoyant work that requires much concentration; cut timber and grub weeds.
Dark of the Moon	When the Moon is within three days of renewal (new) it is at its lowest energy level. Rituals attempted at this time either may produce negative results or not accomplish the intended purposes. Abstain from ritual until the Moon turns new. [9]

The Moon Through the Zodiac

When you devise your own lunar rites, along with the above information you may wish to consider the influence of the Moon as it relates to the signs of the zodiac.

During its twenty-eight-day journey around the Earth, the Moon moves rapidly through the divisions of the sky known as the twelve signs of the zodiac. It spends about two and one-half days in each sign. While it is positioned in a sign, the Moon acquires the sign's characteristics and intensifies its influence on earth. When you plan a ritual, I advise you to check both the phase and the astrological sign the Moon is traversing, so that you can organize the content of your ritual more effectively. (The pertinent data is readily available in any astrological calendar, such as those published by Llewellyn or Jim Maynard.) Bear in mind, too, that during the first and last several hours that the Moon is in a sign, it is considered to be "on a cusp" and receives some influence from the previous or following sign.

As I discussed in my first book, from the time the Moon passes its last aspect to another heavenly body while in a particular sign until it enters the next sign it is in a transition, what astrologers call "void of course." At this time its influence is vague, and the results of any ritual undertaken then could prove counterproductive, unpredictable, or even negative. False starts, delays, and errors all mark the void-of-course period. Therefore, I advise you to refrain from executing any ritual until the Moon moves into the next sign. A good astrological calendar like Jim Maynard's "Celestial Influences" will let you know when the Moon is void of course. Or, you can consult an aspectarian, such as ACS Publishing's *American Ephemeris*.[10]

Plan ritual themes to correspond to the characteristics of the signs of the zodiac through which the Moon is passing. See the full and new Moon rites that follow for examples of how to incorporate key words and themes into your own lunar celebrations. Here I include characteristics of the signs, tips for gardening, the types of rituals best performed according to lunar influences, and general lunar effects to help you thoroughly understand the power of each sign and adjust your daily patterns to their ebb and flow.

Moon in Aries

KEYWORDS: energy, beginnings, determination

CHARACTERISTICS: fiery, barren, dry, masculine

GARDENING: Plant onions only; cultivate the earth, destroy weeds.

RITUALS: Work rituals that require strength, determination, and a particularly auspicious beginning. Rituals that aim at love and friendship are also effective now, as they are when the Moon traverses the other fire signs, Leo and Sagittarius.

ADVICE: Seek out new opportunities, jobs, promotions, business ventures, and ambitious projects, especially those which require bold and sudden moves. Expand your horizons and plan for the future. A breakthrough could be near. Enjoy success, good health, exercise, and new friendships. Guard against selfishness, impulsive behavior, thoughtless remarks, and bad temper. Although you can perform highly skilled work, do not attempt to tackle anything which requires patience until the Moon enters Taurus. Guard against head injuries.

Moon in Taurus

KEYWORDS: diligence, dependability, practicality

CHARACTERISTICS: earthy, productive, moist, feminine

GARDENING: Cultivate your garden and plant hardy, leafy crops, such as spinach, kale, and lettuce, and root crops, such as potatoes, carrots, and beets.

RITUALS: During this phase design rituals that necessitate concentration, discretion, and good judgment, as well as rites dealing with job, home, and family. Also rituals to produce supernatural effects or which seek to manifest one's most secret desires are productive, as they are when the Moon is in the other earth signs, Virgo and Capricorn.

ADVICE: Throughout this phase, people tend to be cautious but task-oriented, dependable, and inclined to indulge in self-analysis and to forge resolutions. Refrain from petty, stubborn, or hyper-critical behavior. Check a desire to overindulge in food, drink, or drugs. Rest and protect your health and finances. Eschew arguments. Try to balance your budget!

Moon in Gemini

KEYWORDS: changeability, communication, entertainment

CHARACTERISTICS: airy, barren, dry, masculine

GARDENING: This is not an auspicious time for gardening of any sort.

RITUALS: During this phase, create rituals that concern travel, new interests, communications, education (especially in the fields of arts and letters), and any rites of an unusual nature, as one performs when the Moon passes through the other air signs, Libra and Aquarius.

ADVICE: People tend to be changeable now. Excitement charges the atmosphere, and you are able to break away successfully from old routines. Your life can become a social whirl now if you let it. You may send or receive letters from afar. Curb a tendency toward self-indulgence; try not to scatter your forces. Avoid gossip.

Moon in Cancer

KEYWORDS: sensitivity, fertility, the home

CHARACTERISTICS: watery, fruitful, moist, feminine

GARDENING: This is an excellent phase for most planting and transplanting.

RITUALS: During this phase accomplish rituals centered around fertility of mind and body, birth and rebirth, family and friends. Now, as when the Moon is in the other water signs, Scorpio and Pisces, rituals involving uncrossing or crossing and clairvoyance are favored.

ADVICE: At this time of the month people tend to dream and fantasize more. They seem to require more love, and their feelings can be hurt easily. Avoid susceptibility to flattery, gullibility, and excessive pride. Do not overindulge in food or drink. If you need to start a diet, do so at this time. If you need to perform a task which requires a lot of memorization, now is the time to do it

Moon in Leo

KEYWORDS: power, flair, generosity

CHARACTERISTICS: fiery, barren, dry, masculine

GARDENING: The best activities for the garden now center around cleanup and elimination of weeds and pests.

RITUALS: This is a fine period to perform rituals involving people in power, promotion, and opportunities, as well as spells for romance and to improve one's appearance.

ADVICE: Participate in social activities, entertainment, and anything that demands showmanship and extravagance, because your vitality is high. Change your hairstyle or add something with a flair to your wardrobe. Avoid being pompous or exerting your authority over others. Watch your budget!

Moon in Virgo

KEYWORDS: service, order, health

CHARACTERISTICS: earthy, barren, moist, feminine

GARDENING: Harvest crops and perform animal husbandry; plot your garden and prepare it.

RITUALS: Work rites to help others. Healing spells are most beneficial during this phase.

ADVICE: At home, reorganize closets, tie up loose ends, answer letters, pay bills. Guard against those whom you suspect want to manipulate you, and conversely, refrain from manipulating others or from being hypercritical. Heed health and diet; attend to your inner spiritual needs.

Moon in Libra

KEYWORDS: harmony, beauty, grace

CHARACTERISTICS: airy, semi-fruitful, moist, feminine

GARDENING: Plant flowers and ornamentals.

RITUALS: When the Moon is in Libra, perform rituals that treat interpersonal relationships, particularly romance, unions, and marriages. It is an ideal time to organize and direct the wills of the members of your coven toward a single goal, because a spirit of cooperation and teamwork prevails.

ADVICE: In daily life, instinct and intuition are accurate, and an atmosphere of charm and eloquence dominates. Get involved with the arts, theater and beauty. Partnerships can blossom now. In meditation, endeavor to balance your personality. Curb sarcasm. Important choices may have to be made.

Moon in Scorpio

KEYWORDS: the occult, regeneration, concentration

CHARACTERISTICS: watery, fruitful, moist, masculine

GARDENING: It is an auspicious time to plant and prune. Plant vines now.

RITUALS: Execute rites to draw money, and exercise your innate clairvoyant powers.

ADVICE: Do not let yourself get dragged down by murky thinking, because an atmosphere of jealousy, suspicion, and negativity may prevail. Criticisms levelled at this time will probably be sharp but accurate. During this lunar phase houseclean and rearrange furniture; sink into deep meditational states using black candles as an aid. This is a good time to accomplish personal detective work.

Moon in Sagittarius

KEYWORDS: stimulation, humanity, intellect

CHARACTERISTICS: fiery, barren, dry, masculine

GARDENING: As when the Moon is in all the fire signs except Aries, do not plant anything now.

RITUALS: Perform rituals that require self-directed energy. Work Magic to attain your highest goals. Rites to enable you to write or to encourage publication of materials already written are effective. Work now to heal animals, especially horses.

ADVICE: It is an opportune time to seek mental and emotional stimulation through the study of philosophy and theology, or foreign travel. Pursue outdoor activities. During this phase the atmosphere is charged with expectation. People tend to be candid with one another, but in a good-humored way, each manifesting intrinsic humanitarian instincts.

Moon in Capricorn

KEYWORDS: ambition, dignity, responsibility

CHARACTERISTICS: earthy, productive, dry, feminine

GARDENING: Plant root and other sturdy crops now.

RITUALS: During this phase, accomplish rituals that need an extra impetus to set them in motion. It is an auspicious time for rites involving career, honors, personal advancement, old plans, removal of obstacles, and acquisition of material goods, particularly homes.

ADVICE: Be especially kind to older people; curb ambition, pessimism, and any tendency toward cruelty. Moderate your activities. Treat others with respect.

Moon in Aquarius

KEYWORDS: imagination, synthesis, sharing

CHARACTERISTICS: airy, barren, dry, masculine

GARDENING: Not recommended for planting.

RITUALS: When the Moon traverses Aquarius, perform rituals to improve the intellect, or rites that develop the imagination and require an innovative approach. Try to get together with a group to perform Magic now; the results will be electrifying.

ADVICE: People tend to be philosophically and intellectually inclined and are more sociable during this phase. It is an excellent time to consult an astrologer. However, avoid making unrealistic plans. Expect the unexpected!

Moon in Pisces

KEYWORDS: perception, self-sacrifice, spirituality

CHARACTERISTICS: watery, fruitful, moist, feminine

GARDENING: Almost anything planted at this time will flourish.

RITUALS: With the Moon in Pisces, forge ahead on rituals for psychic work and development.

ADVICE: During meditation, endeavor to gain personal insights into your character flaws. Your dreams may be prophetic. Avoid vagueness of expression, deception, self-deception, self-indulgence, and the feeling that you are a martyr. It is the worst time to experiment with drugs.

Full Moon Healers' Ritual

Wicca practices and beliefs vary widely, but all Witches seem to perceive themselves as healers, or strive to become healers. One reason why Witches develop their psychic gifts is their commitment to healing the body, mind, and spirit of all living entities on Earth. The following full-Moon ritual affirms the desire to heal and develop healing energy.

It is appropriate either as a group or solo rite. Perform the ritual when the Moon is near full or full, and in Virgo.

Items Required

A white or violet altar cloth; white altar candles dressed with narcissus oil; Wings of Healing incense; burner, coal and matches; milk-and-honey offering to Demeter in an earthen bowl; roses on the altar; rosemary with which to ring the Circle; salt with which to draw a sigil; straw and a few strands of blond hair, corn silk, or straw for the "Apollo tresses"; a crystal point for each covener; heliotrope oil; medicine bag or box; paints or embroidery materials to decorate the medicine bag or box (explained below).

At this ritual you will begin to assemble and fill your medicine bag. Since it is a personal tool that reflects your individual personality and healing talents, it can take many forms. Buy a leather pouch, sew a silk bag, or select a small box. The size is a matter of personal preference, as is how many items you wish to store in it. Collect twelve to twenty items, including healing stones, healing sands, herbal mixtures, herbs, barks, sigils, etc.

The bag or box can be white for purity and astral light, yellow for Solar Magic, blue for Lunar Magic, orange for Mercury energy and healing, red for Mars energy and life, or violet for refined healing vibrations. Decorate the bag or box with symbols related to health, such as the astrological signs for Sun, Mercury, or Virgo and your own sign; the names Hamaliel (spirit of Virgo), Raphael (god as healer), Ormuz (spirit of good); or roses, poppies, violets, a bee, a torch, etc. Paint or embroider these symbols on the box or bag. If you use a bag, string crystal beads or other healing stones along the drawstring. Personally, I prefer a box lined with orange silk, which I find practical because I can compartmentalize my healing paraphernalia so that items are easy to find.

For the ritual you need not have decided every detail of the bag's decoration, nor each item you will want to put in the bag. Have an idea in mind of at least one element of the design to decorate during the ritual. As to the talismans, you will add only the Apollo's tresses and crystal at this time. Later, as you find them, you can include more healing devices; decorate the outside with more adornments as you think of them until you feel your healing bag is complete.

Preparations

Erect the altar in the East, and cover it with the white or violet cloth. Place the two anointed altar candles on each side toward the back, with the roses between them. The heliotrope oil goes to the front left side of the altar; the bowl of milk and honey goes to the front and center.

A covener other than the Priestess (if this is a group rite) sprinkles rosemary around the Circle and traces the following sigil (figure 8) with salt in the center of the Circle. The sigil should be large enough so that all the crystals can be placed on top of it for charging. Place several lighted white candles and

Figure 8: Healing Sigil for the Full-Moon Healer's Ritual

consecrated symbols of the elements (incense, red candle, water, salt) at the Quarters. Burn Wings of Healing incense in the East.

The Rite

The Priestess opens the Circle in the usual manner, and then invokes Demeter, the Virgoan goddess of the Earth.

INVOCATION TO DEMETER

Priestess: "Corn-crowned goddess, heart of the earth, you who carries the torch that lights the Circle of never-ending life, mother of Persephone, I call you to this sacred ground to lend your power to our rite. Mother Mountain, enfold us in your earth-hewn walls, and protect us from the rigors of the long and frozen night. Lend us the key that unlocks the secret of your strength and stability.

"In gratitude for all you bestow upon us we offer you this sweet and mellifluous product of your bounty."

The Priestess takes the bowl of milk and honey and sprinkles some on the ground in front of the altar, first to the left, to the right, and then to the center.

INVOCATION OF APOLLO

The Priest, (or if no male is present, a female covener who assumes the role of the Priest) invokes Apollo: "Embodiment of light, son of Zeus and Leto, twin of Artemis, mystical illumination, you who proceeds from the depths of the lion, you I invoke to empower our Circle with the regenerating rays of the Sun. Bathe us in your healing warmth so that we may convey your power to those in need."

AFFIRMATION: INTENT TO BECOME HEALERS

Priestess: "Tonight we all are drawn together into this bright refuge from the storms that ravage the outer darkness with a single purpose. Tonight the Moon traverses Virgo, sign of health, medicine and service, and the Virgin's influence manifests around us. Our desire, our goal, our responsibility as Witches is to heal others with the divine knowledge imparted to us. Let our bodies, as temples of the Light, be unsullied vessels ready to receive the power of the

Light and transmit it purely and fully to other living beings.

"We henceforth vow to do everything in our power to prepare ourselves to be perfect conductors, to touch others with the rejuvenating force of the Light, having no other aim in mind than to serve Love Divine."

All: "So mote it be! Blessed Be!"

RITE OF APOLLO'S TRESSES

Coveners bring forth their medicine bags, pouches, boxes, etc., and sit in a circle around the healer's sigil that has been drawn on the ground with salt. They embroider or paint a symbol evocative of healing on their bags or boxes, and take strands of straw, cornsilk, or hair, and braid them together into Apollo's tresses. If you count among your group a natural blond, she may wish to donate a few strands of hair to work into the braids. When finished, place the braids into the containers.

Use Apollo's tresses to psychically sweep away dis-ease and negativity from patients' auras.

CHARGING THE CRYSTALS

Crystals are excellent accumulators; they have the capacity to capture and hold any influence directed toward them. If you charge your crystal with the intent to heal, you can extract the power later by force of will, and divert it to a patient. Charging the crystals in Circle intensifies their healing energy because several wills combine toward this single purpose. Even if you perform this rite solo, your crystal will be powerfully charged because you will tap into divine healing energy that will be focused by the sigil.

After the initial charging, you should continue to charge the crystal during Waxing Moon meditations. The more energy you put into it the more you will get out. Whenever you need to unlock its power, perform a ritual where you mentally envision the healing power as a pinpoint of light deep within the crystal, which you lengthen and draw from its source as a brilliant ray. Will the ray to enter your head at your third eye, and to flow through your body and out your fingers toward the object of the healing.

To perform the charging of the crystals you and the other coveners first anoint your crystal points with heliotrope oil. Place the crystals in the center of the healing sigil.

Next, link hands around the Circle and chant *EH-VO-HE* to build a cone of power. If you wish, as long as hands remain linked, you can dance around the Circle faster and faster. When the cone is raised and the chant is at its strongest, stop dancing and chanting, release hands, and direct the energy toward the crystals. The crystals are now charged and ready to go into the medicine bags.

Thanksgiving and Closing of Circle

Priest: "We thank the healing spirits for attending this rite and lending their energy to its success. We understand that along with the power to heal that has been bestowed upon us comes great responsibility, and we promise never to abuse our gift. As healers we will work always within the Light."

The Priestess closes the Circle in the usual manner. As you return to the mundane plane, may your hearts be lighter, and may your being be filled with infinite joy.

New Moon Ritual

To Gain an Understanding of Fire and to Undertake New Projects

(MOON IN ARIES)

All ye that kindle a fire, that compass yourselves about with spirits, walk in the light of your fire, and in the sparks that ye have kindled. [11]

Introduction

While the full Moon is the time during which most constructive rituals take place, your coven can also harness the energy of the new Moon. The new Moon phase is a good time to perform rituals for undertaking new projects and to spur the members of the coven to accomplish their highest aims. The following ritual offers a variation on these themes.

New Moon in Aries is a time to begin new projects and adventures, because Aries energy sparks plans with the impetus they need to be brought to fruition. This lunar phase is given to mental, emotional, and physical stimulation; it is a time when you can throw aside the obstacles in your path and make breakthroughs in the struggle to achieve your highest aspirations. Sometimes unusual or unplanned events can occur. Since Aries is a fire sign, it embraces the idea of transmutation. It also encompasses both the positive and negative poles of fire. On one hand, it is vital and warm, emanating nourishing light and heat; on the other, it is a purifying and destructive force that consumes impetuously and indiscriminately everything in its wake. Prior to the ritual, when meditating on images of fire, attempt to unite your energy with that of fire at both the levels of animal passion and spiritual strength; for this is the key to tapping the power of the duality of fire.

Items Required
A red or orange altar cloth, embroidered with fire tattvas; Vesta Fire incense;

Figure 9: Fire Wheel

burner, coal, and matches; red altar candles anointed with Invocation oil; a fire laid in a fireplace or wood stove, or needfire mix in a cauldron; a swastika (fire wheel, or blazing cross, symbol of the power of fire in motion) (see figure 9) painted in orange on a red background over a cardboard circle which you place on the altar; a straw figure basted with a mixture of honey and vesta powder; bay salt and frankincense powder to throw into the fire during the divination; whole wild ginger pieces in a bowl on the altar as an offering to the elemental spirits of fire.

EVOCATION OF THE SALAMANDERS, ELEMENTAL SPIRITS OF FIRE
The Priestess opens the Circle in the usual manner. Another covener stands before the altar and raises the bowl of ginger as an offering to the elemental spirits of fire. He addresses the elements.

Covener: "Spirits of fire, elusive salamanders who dance in the flame, you who are the mediators between forms, you who are pure desire in motion; Paralda, King of the Sylphs, I beckon you to attend our ritual. To entice you forth, I tender unto you this offering of wild and spicy ginger."

INVOCATION OF VESTA, GODDESS OF THE HEARTH FIRE
Priestess: "Lady of the hearth fire, keeper of the sacred flame, you from whom all things proceed and to whom they return, you who are the purifier of spiritual energy and renewer of all nature, I invoke you, white-clad goddess, Vesta, to enter our Circle of Light. Focus your pure and penetrating ray on our humble home fire."

INVOCATION OF BALDER, THE FIRE GOD
Priest: "Radiant god of innocence, wisdom, and light; Balder the Beautiful, Balder the Good, you whose snowy brow and gold-kissed tresses radiate the bright beams that nurture all life; Sun God, I call you forth to grace our Circle with your joyful presence."

AFFIRMATION
Priestess: "We are here tonight to tap the free-flowing energy of Aries, and to

bring the strength and wisdom of the divine fire to our sphere. May we, like a candle's flame, sway to the impulses of life, and adapt ourselves to the rhythm of vitality. Yet may we never let our most cherished desires and goals disappear from sight and be extinguished."

Rite of the Wall of Light

In this segment of the ritual, the coveners gather in a circle and visualize that they are inducing the Universal Light into their bodies. They shape the Light to flow around them like a circular wall through which no evil or negativity may penetrate from the outside. The wall acts like a two-way mirror, and although no evil may enter through the wall, the coveners may push out through the wall any negative thoughts that obstruct their goals. When they have finished, they transform the wall of light into a fog and dissolve it. All is accomplished with oral encouragement from the Priestess and chanting.

Priestess: "We shall now build the Wall of Light. Sit comfortably in the Circle and face inwards. Some of you may wish to cross your legs yogi style. Shake your bodies to loosen them, and begin rhythmic breathing. At the sound of the bell, we will begin to draw to us the Universal Light.

"Ready? Breathe in, 1—2—3—4. Out, 4—3—2—1. Again."

The Priestess repeats the instructions at least six times, then rings a bell.

Priestess: "I want you to tap into the universal fluid of Light and direct it down into your bodies from the tops of your heads. The Light is radiant; the Light is transparent white; the Light is electric! Let its rays fill your bodies as a chalice with sparkling white wine. Fill your bodies to the brim with pure, radiant White Light.

"When you feel your body brimming to capacity, hold out your hands in front of you, and will the Light to flow like electricity from your fingertips. Move the stream of Light over your head and behind you, where it merges with rays from the other coveners, and builds a formidable Wall of Light.

"Stronger and stronger it flows, until the Light begins to vibrate, pulsate, and move as a body. Around and around it slowly rotates in a circle from left to right. Around and around, and around some more. Slowly increasing its speed as you chant *AUM MANE PADME HUM.*"

The coveners and the Priestess begin to chant. As the chant intensifies, the Priestess recites the following.

Priestess: "Light be with me. Light within me. Light behind me. Light before me, Light beside me, Light to win me, Light to comfort and restore me. Light beneath me, Light above me, Light in quiet, Light in danger, Light in hearts of all that love me, Light in mind of friend and stranger. *AUM MANE PADME HUM. AUM MANE PADME HUM. AUM MANE PADME HUM!*"

Everyone stops chanting and drops hands.

Priestess: "I want you to contemplate your divine aim, the goal that you are most determined to achieve. See it as a star twinkling in the heavens. Think of all the obstacles to your goal, everything that obstructs your path to achievement. One by one, push back the obstacles through the Wall of Light behind you and out into the cosmos. Push the obstacles out through the Wall, and they will never return. They will never bother you again."

After several minutes the Priestess rings the bell and says, "It is time to dissolve the Wall of Light. The Light grows dense and opaque, it becomes dimmer, like a fog. Heavy and hazy, it is now a fog. Yet the fog dims and becomes a mist, and soon begins to dissipate. The mist is like a lattice. Slowly it dissolves into space and disappears. The Light has returned to its source."

Pyromancy

The Priest lights the fire and brings out the straw doll.

Priest: "As this straw doll, symbol of our questions about the future, is consumed in the flame, may each of us see true and gain insight into our inquiries."

The Priest tosses the doll upon the flame, another covener throws in the bay salt, and another the frankincense powder, and everyone seeks a message in the flames. After several minutes, the Priest rings the bell to arouse the coveners from their reveries.

Closing the Circle

The Priestess thanks and banishes spirits in the usual manner. The rite is ended.

After a fire ritual people usually retain a good deal of energy. Therefore your group might want to participate in some lively dancing. A Scottish reel is appropriately thematic, because it is an ancient Celtic creation dance.

Tips on Pyromancy

In order to help you with the pyromancy part of the ritual, I include here some traditional portents that may be divined by fire.

Positive Signs
* The fire burns vigorously and quickly consumes the doll
* The fire burns transparently and clearly, burning blue or yellow
* The fire burns brightly or glowing—wealth, happiness, cheerfulness, longevity
* The flames leap—they are about to talk
* The fire burns silently in a pyramidal form

Negative Signs
* The fire is difficult to kindle, or slow to consume the doll
* The fire burns dark or red—sinister forces roam abroad
* The flames crackle—a warning; all is not as it seems
* The flame is suddenly extinguished—disaster
* The flame bends—the healthy will fall ill; the sick will die

Fire Symbols

The following meanings of symbols represent a few of the images that may be glimpsed in the fire. The significances are traditional.

abbey—consolation from worries; a hiatus in activities
airplane—travel, success
anchor—true love, security
army on the march—a great event is foreshadowed

baby—good luck in the home; problems will not last long
banner—glory and honor
beans—money troubles, grave danger
bear—an awkward friend
bed—you need a vacation; unmade bed—disorder, a mistake
bee—success in career
bell—a wedding, good news
boat—good news, happiness; labor will bear fruit
bones—catastrophe
bridge—take a chance, because you will reach a happy solution
broom—you will make a change
bushes—triumph over obstacles
candle—spiritual growth; lighted—birth; extinguished—death
castle—a happy event
cavern—great sorrow
chain—sorrow, suffering
circle—reconciliation
clouds -a quarrel, threats
cradle—birth; hope is realized
crab—separation
cross—you are protected
crown—vanity, honor
cup—love, union
devil—torment, peril
dog—a faithful friend
doll—ephemeral pleasure
dragon—obstacles
egg—a new development, a new plan
face—smiling—happiness, long life; sad—worry, idleness
farm animals—good news about money
feather—frivolity, needless fretting
fish—happiness, joy, success

flag—change, success
flowers—white—worry, grief; red—good health; faded— disappointment
flying birds—letters
fox—success
ghost—someone from the past is looking for you; white—joy; black—
sorrow
goose—insincerity
hat—change of residence, disillusionment
hammer—imprudence
heart—friendship turns to love
hen—white—festivity; black—woe
horse—journey; a good omen
house—better times are ahead
hut—solitude, isolation
island—abandonment, isolation
key—secret to be revealed
kite—frustrated desires
knife—danger, peril
ladder—success through perserverance
leaves—changes; budding—birth; dead—bad news
lion—a powerful person
lighthouse—protection
monk—success through prayer
Moon—money, travel
mountain—your friends will help you
nails—unexpected news
nest—good luck
owl—delay action for a while
pipe—comfort, satisfaction
rainbow—troubles will end soon
rat—unknown enemies
ring—marriage, reconciliation

scissors—separation

shoe—new—consolation; old—sadness

snake—someone bears you a grudge

spider—a lawsuit is afoot

star—happiness, success

Sun—good fortune, triumph

sword—victory after tremendous effort

table—abundance, comfort, blessings

tiger—danger

toad—danger; fertility

torch—happiness, enlightenment

tree—an auspicious time for new undertakings; felled—loss; fruiting—prosperity

umbrella—open—protection, aid; shut—success in business

violin—love blooms

volcano—dangerous adventure

wheel—one who is away will return soon; a change in fortune for the better

window—open—success; shut—escape from danger

wine—a happy, vigorous old age

wolf—triumph

Chapter Three
The Elements

Imagine our prehistoric ancestors huddled around a fire in their frozen, mist-enshrouded caves, teeth chattering with terror and cold, listening to the wind howl and the rain lash the trees outside. No wonder they feared, respected, and even worshipped the elements of Air, Fire, Water, and Earth! Throughout the tedious, lightless winters, our predecessors devised entertaining stories about the elements and personalized their powers in order to make sense of the awesome forces of nature that controlled human lives. In this way they created the enchanting lore about the elements, their rulers, minions, and elemental spirits.

Our antecedents lived much closer to nature than we do now, and in their myths about the elementals lies a good deal of truth about the forces that the elements represent. Before you attempt to contact them and use the elemental forces, I suggest you review the qualities that follow.

Air

The Midnight Wind

O! I could laugh to hear the midnight wind,
That, rushing on its way with careless sweep,

Scatters the ocean waves. And I could weep
Like to a child. For now to my raised mind
On wings of winds comes wild-eyed Phantasy.
And her rude visions give severe delight.
O winged bark! how swift along the night
Pass'd thy proud keel! nor shall I let go by
Lightly of that drear hour the memory,
When wet and chilly on the deck I stood,
Unbonneted, and gazed upon the flood,
Even till it seemed a pleasant thing to die, —
To be resolv'd into the elemental wave,
Or take my portion with the winds that rave.

Charles Lamb *(1775 - 1834)*

Considered the primary element out of which all else proceeds, Air is the essence of motion. In a word, it signifies mutability, the meaning of which is complex. We speak of the "breath of life," the *prana,* or vital principle out of which we all are formed. We also think of Air as encompassing the space which is a medium for movement, and out of which life forms proceed. J.E. Cirlot in *A Dictionary of Symbols* sums the notions involved in the principle of air thus:

> Air is essentially related to three sets of ideas: the creative breath of life, and hence, speech; the stormy wind, connected in many mythologies with the idea of creation; and finally, space as a medium for movement and for the emergence of life-processes.[12]

When we contemplate the mutability of Air, the idea of change springs to mind—change which in itself is the only thing that endures. Concepts associated with Air include light, scent, freedom, flight, wind, climate, and atmosphere. The Magicians of old classified Air as active, hot, moist, and light. The element is embodied in Hermes, the winged god of communication, human thought, dance, flexibility, thievery, medicine, and learning. The elemental tattva is Vayu, the blue circle, and the direction of the wind (in Northern

European and American traditions) is from the East, ruled by Notus. The Archangel is Raphael, the healer god. The elusive elementals of Air, called sylphs, are ruled by their king, Paralda. The athame, symbol of the Magician's life force and primary ritual tool, belongs to the element. By tradition, Witches controlled the movement of Air and "whistled up the wind" by going outside at dawn and letting go with three shrill bursts of sound in the direction from where they wanted the wind to blow. Such feats were much in demand with sailors, who paid dearly for the service. Witches still divine the future in the messages borne by the voices of the wind. They use the energy of Air to perform astral travel and to find objects that have been stolen.

One of the most "spirited" representations I have seen of the element Air is the British rock musical performed on roller skates, *Starlight Express.* In this show, the character of the electric train, AC-DC, expertly embodies the motion, elusiveness, changeability, and weightlessness of Air.

Fire

Into the Magick Fire all things are cast. It symbolizes the final burning up of all things in Shivandarshana. It is the absolute destruction alike of the Magician and the Universe.[13]

Fire stands for transmutation. We speak of "trial by fire" to mean transcendence and renewal. Fire is a powerful element, capable of both generating and purifying life and of destroying it. It is the element that operates at the center of all things. I associate the tarot card the Tower with Fire. Although the Tower is rent by lightning bolts and disintegrates in the flames that consume it, from its crumbled foundation, the Tower is soon rebuilt on a firmer basis.

Other characteristics of Fire include heat, light, motion, control, protection, and vengeance. Magicians categorize Fire as hot and dry, light and active. Its ritual instruments are the fire-stick, or power wand, symbol of the Magician's will, and the lamp. The Archangel of the element is Michael, known as "the strong one of god"; the elemental spirits, named salamanders, are presided over by Djinn; god forms comprise any of the sun gods such as Lugh, Baal, Balder, and Horus. The wind that blows from the south is named Euros. The tattva to contemplate is Tejas, the red triangle.

Witches use Fire for pyromancy and Alchemy; they celebrate its power with the needfire and bonfires.

Water

Mountain Lakes
"The calm green lakes are sleeping in the mountain shadow, and on the water's canvas bright sunshine paints the picture of the day."[14]

The Mountain Stream
"Mountain stream, clear and limpid, wandering down towards the valley, whispering songs among the rushes —oh, that I were as the stream!" [15]

The Storm
"Cold is the night in the Great Moor, the rain pours down, no trifle; a roar in which the clean wind rejoices howls over the sheltering wood." [16]

So many concepts are associated with Water that it is difficult to sum its influence in a word. But if I were to choose one, it would be love, infinite and divine—an all-pervasive, overwhelming feeling experienced on this plane perhaps only by those who have survived near-death experiences.

Among the many concepts expressed by Water are: the tides, the unconscious mind, emotions, receptivity, fertility, compassion, creativity, fluidity, intuition, transparency, the limitless, and the ineffable. Water is considered cold and moist, heavy and passive; the direction of its wind is west, and is named Zephyr. The Archangel is Gabriel; the elementals, the Undines, are ruled by Niksa. The Witch's water tool is the chalice, and Apas, the silver crescent, composes the tattvic symbol.

Today, as in days of old, people still drop offerings into wishing wells as testaments to their belief in the subtle influence of Water over their lives. Water was once thought to be the *prima materia* from which life was engendered. It even was considered the mediator between life and death.

Witches work Water Magic by gazing into magic mirrors, cups, or cauldrons full of water. By harnessing the power of Water, they are able to raise storms at sea, heal the body, and make it fertile, and perform Dream Magic on the astral plane. A key water deity is Albion.

Earth

A Ballad for Trolls

We are the trolls; we like the night.
We hate churchbells, gun powder, dynamite.
We fear sunlight.

We bear the tag of the devil; we are outcast Lilith's brood,
without souls, the churchfolk say, and cannot love the Good.

Our eyesight is splintered; our logic's so askew, we think
it fine to dine on cow cakes, drink our oxen's own home-brew.

Beltane fires enrage us; Balder's Balefire built at crossroads
make us run.
The rood and the mistletoe spoil our fun.
Speak our names and we are stunned.
We turn to stone if we look at the sun.

We have no wits, so cannot win;
but without souls, how can we sin?
Who covets Earth is our kin.
We are Trolls. [17]

The element Earth represents the physical plane of manifestation. This is the realm of stability and strength, protection and hidden knowledge. Magicians conceived of the Earth as cold and dry, heavy and passive. The name of the north wind is Boreas, Auriel is the Archangel of the Quarter, and the elemental spirits, the gnomes, are led by their king, Ghob. Tools of the element include the pentacle and the crystal. Finally, the tattvic symbol is Prithivi, the yellow square.

Witches use Earth energy to seek directional guidance and practice herb, oil, and gem Magic, runecasting, geomancy, and knot magic. The Earth Mother is considered the force behind the expression of Earth energies.

Now that you are familiar with the qualities of the elements, you can meditate on them in order to explore their depths and draw them to you in order to strengthen and balance your personality. The following water meditation gives you an idea of how to proceed. Choose the proper setting, and organize the meditation around the salient characteristics of each element that you wish to understand and incorporate into your being.

Meditation on the Element Water

"Strong and free, strong and free,
The floodgates are open, away to the sea,
Free and strong, free and strong,

Cleansing my streams as I hurry along,
To the golden sands, and the leaping bar,
And the taintless tide that awaits me afar—
As I lose myself in the infinite main,
Like a soul that has sinned and is pardoned again.
Undefiled, for the undefiled;
Play by me, bathe in me, mother and child."[18]

Items Required

A warm bathroom with a bathtub, sink, and warm water; two silver or blue candles anointed with Rising Moon oil and candleholders; Egyptian hieroglyph of water, consisting of three wavy lines (symbolizing the primeval ocean) painted on a circular piece of strong cardboard in silver on a blue background bordered with sea green (figure 10); Moon Mistress bath salts; towels; emollients; a bath pillow, if desired.

Preparations

In this meditation you will attempt to contact the elemental spirits of water by taking a ritual bath, focusing on a hieroglyphic symbol of the element water, and reading the guided meditation.

Undoubtedly you already have developed a ritualized, personal procedure for bathing. So, while the following suggestions may be useful, you may wish to ignore them or modify them to conform to your routine.

Take a quick shower to remove surface dirt and apply emollients to your elbows, knees, and other dry spots. Draw a warm (90 - 98 degree) bath. Lay out the towels and emollients. Place the hieroglyph on the faucets against the wall, with the lighted candles on either side. Adjust the bath pillow so that you can lean back comfortably in the tub. Add the Moon Mistress bath salts to the water. Adjust the water in the sink so that it drips slightly. If you have a large, smooth stone, place it in the basin so that the water drips over it. To ease yourself into a meditative state, play background music evocative of the water deities. I suggest the *Nature Meditation* by Lady Sara Cunningham-Carter.

Now relax in the tub for several minutes. Re-read the section of this chapter on Water, and the poem from *The Water Babies*.

Perform the Banishing and Invoking Pentagrams of Water that you learned from the Greater Pentagram Ritual in chapter 1. Imagine your body as a hollow vessel surrounded by all the water in the world. Then, as you read aloud the following invocation, cause your body to yield to the pressure of the water, and absorb the liquid into the hollow spaces.

Figure 10: Water Meditation Sigil

Invocation to the Undines

"Transparencies floating in the limitless void,
Formless, unfathomable and fluid...
Pearl-gray fascinators of the ancient twilight,
Undines, spirits of Water,
I call you forth!
Emerge from the silvery stream of life
And appear before me.
Come, enter me now, and share with me your essence.

Cleanse and regenerate my spirit!"

Now, sit back and contemplate the hieroglyph. Presently, the undines will appear to you, and perhaps bring you a message. When you are ready to end the meditation, perform the Banishing Pentagram of Water. As you do so, visualize the excess water that entered the hollows of your body drain back into the tub. Despatch the elementals with the following:

"Niksa, king of the undines,
Albion of my heart,
Gabriel, image of god,
I thank you for permitting me to spend this time with you and experience your essence. May we go our separate ways now, you, back to your formless, limitless realm, I to my solid, earthly abode. I am ever enriched by the knowledge you have shared with me. Elemental spirits of water, until again we meet, hail and farewell!"

Open the drain in the tub before you step out of the water. In that way, you symbolically will any impurities to drain from you before you leave the meditation site.

The Planets

When the Moon is in the seventh house
And Jupiter aligns with Mars
Then peace will guide our planet
And love will rule the stars[19]

In a 7-11 convenience store recently I picked up at the counter, along with a candy bar, my monthly horoscope. Neatly and tightly wrapped in a little tube, it looked like a cigarette until I unrolled it. These days, horoscopes are carried by most newspapers and are avidly read alongside the comics. People as different as financial wizards, actors, and housewives regularly consult astrologers to plan their daily activities. All this attests to the widespread popularity of astrology and the worldwide belief that the planets somehow affect our lives. Exactly what are the influences of the planets and how can their power be brought to bear in rituals?

The planets as we know them are the heavenly bodies in our solar system: Mercury, Venus, Mars, Jupiter, Saturn, Neptune, Uranus, and Pluto. The Sun and the Moon, although not true planets, are included in the categorization because of their undeniable influence on the Earth. Over time, observers discovered the particular influences of the planets by watching the sky and noting the positions of planets when certain events occurred on Earth. A belief evolved that planetary movements mirror larger cosmic movements that affect life on Earth.

Ancient astrologers charted the positions of the planets at the moment of a person's birth and their subsequent movements in the sky to help them cast horoscopes that described a newborn's character, personality, and expectations.

The Magicians of old delved deeply into the influences of the planets and developed a set of symbols, or correspondences, to describe the planets' effects. These correspondences extended to colors, seasons, perfumes, metals, incense, woods, musical tones, animals, plants, precious stones, god forms, numbers, days of the week, etc. Since early Magicians did not know about the existence of Neptune, Uranus and Pluto, correspondences for these planets were worked out later, and consequently, are less comprehensive.

Whether you decide to interpret the significance of the planets as actual or symbolic, their influence is strong and undeniable. In rituals, Witches may draw upon a planetary force to put them in a proper frame of mind to perform a ritual, or they may plan entire rites centered around a specific planetary influence.

The Magi

The Magicians of times gone by took their planetary rites seriously and carried out elaborate preparations for them. Usually they established a permanent temple that they embellished with the signs and symbols of each heavenly body, including the appropriate colors, gemstones, metals, representations of gods and goddesses, flowers, herbs, perfumes, incense, and other symbols. The splendidly robed and crowned Magician then stepped onto a painted circle etched with magical names, and invoked the spirits with his magic wand or sword. The forces he conjured manifested within the Magic Triangle prepared with the written signature or sigil of the spirit. After the spirits appeared and were persuaded to do the conjurer's bidding, the Magician banished them to their celestial abodes.

Today you still can learn to invoke the spirits of the planetary realms (the raw energy forces that pulsate throughout the Cosmos), cause them to manifest on this plane, and command them to work your will.

The following list of planetary correspondences will help you to achieve this aim. Gather around your Magic Circle as many of the correspondences as possible before you perform the rite. The more symbols of the designated planetary force you can muster, the better the likelihood of success. The correspondences both carry inherent values and serve to put you in the appropriate state of mind to merge your imagination with the planetary force. The right use of imagination is your principal aim for bringing off any ritual; all depends on your and the Divine Will. For a model of how to prepare, construct, and perform a planetary ritual, see the Rite of Mercury that follows the list of planetary characteristics.

Planetary Characteristics and Associations

SUN

DAY: Sunday
GENDER: masculine
NUMBER: 6

DIRECTION: north

COLORS: gold, yellow, white, orange.

GEMSTONES: diamond; carbuncle; cat's eye; chrysolite; jacinth; topaz.

METAL: gold

GOD/DESS FORMS: Adonis; Apollo; Baal; Horus; Jehovah; Daath; Lugh; Ra

CREATURES: child; lion; phoenix

SYMBOL: solar disc or wheel

DOMICILE: Leo

DETRIMENT: Aquarius

EXALTATION: Aries

FALL: Libra

GOD NAME: Jehova Eloah-ve-Daath

ARCHANGEL: Michael

ANGEL: Shinanim

SPIRIT: Och (Sorath)

INTELLIGENCE: Nachiel

SEPHIRA: Tiphareth (Beauty)

TAROT CARD: The Sun (XIX)

FLOWERS: forsythia; goldenrod; heliotrope; juniper; marigold; peony; pimpernel; poppy; sunflower; saffron

INCENSE: benzoin; calamus; camphor; frankincense; mastic; myrrh; red santal; storax

PERFUMES: cinnamon; clove; frankincense; heliotrope; myrrh

PLANTS: aloes; angelica; bay laurel; burnet; celadine; centaury; chamomile; clove; corn; dandelion; datura; eyebright; heart trefoil; juniper; lovage; meadow rue; mistletoe; orange; pineapple; rice; rosemary; rue; saffron; St. Johnswort; spearmint; storax

WOODS: acacia; almond; ash; bay; chicory; laurel; lignum vitae; walnut

TIME: early adulthood

NEGATIVE EFFECTS ON PERSONALITY: self-centeredness; pride; despotism; boastfulness; pomposity; ostentation

PARTS OF THE BODY: right eye; pituitary and thyroid glands; heart; spine; spleen

TONE: D

LETTER: S

RITUAL THEMES: health; healing; revitalization; harmony; spiritual cleansing; career advancement; promotions; politics; fast luck; prosperity; finances; recovery of lost property; ideals; one's destiny; self-confidence; hope; friendship; peace; the Qabala.

MOON

DAY: Monday

GENDER: feminine

NUMBER: 9

DIRECTION: west

COLORS: silver; white; pale blue; pale green; violet

GEMSTONES: crystal; moonstone; pearl; quartz

METALS: aluminum; silver

GOD/DESS FORMS: Diana; Hecate; Isis; Khensu; Luna; Morrighan; Selene

CREATURES: cow; doe; elephant; goose

SYMBOLS: archer; huntress

DOMICILE: Cancer

DETRIMENT: Capricorn

EXALTATION: Taurus

FALL: Scorpio

GOD NAME: Shaddai el Chai

ARCHANGEL: Gabriel

ANGELS: Ishim; Cherubim

SPIRITS: Chasmodai; Phul

INTELLIGENCE: Malkiel

SEPHIRA: Yesod (Foundation)

TAROT CARD: High Priestess (II)

FLOWERS: daisy; forget-me-not; honeysuckle; iris; jasmine; lily-of-the-valley; peony; wallflower; white poppy

INCENSE: aloes; bay leaf; camphor myrrh; myrtle leaf

PERFUMES: honeysuckle; iris; jasmine; lily-of-the-valley; peony; white sandal-wood

PLANTS: arrowhead; banana; bay; betony; cabbage; chickwood; clary sage; coralwort; cucumber; endive; fleur-de-lis; lettuce; melino; moonwort; mugwort; mushroom; myrtle; pennyroyal; opium poppy; pumpkin; purslane; seaweed; trefoil (clover); watercress; white poppy; white rose; wintergreen; wormwood; yellow flag; all vegetable leaves

WOODS: almond; cedar; hazel; juniper; willow

TIME: infancy

NEGATIVE EFFECTS ON PERSONALITY: inability to decipher one's own feelings; over-reaction; hypersensitivity

PARTS OF THE BODY: breast; right eye; esophagus; pituitary and thyroid glands; lymph glands; nervous system; medula; ovaries; uterus

TONE: F

LETTER: R

RITUAL THEMES: astral travel; psychic shields; safety in travel; reconciliation; housecleaning; and other domestic matters; fertility; birth; maternity; emotions; imagination; security; Water Magic; femininity; medicine; viruses; stomach and blood disorders; protection; reversal of negativity; prophecy; vulnerability; romance; fascination; and of course; Moon Magic

MARS

DAY: Tuesday

GENDER: masculine

NUMBER: 5

DIRECTION: east

COLORS: red; orange

GEMSTONES: bloodstone; garnet; ruby

METALS: iron; steel

SYMBOLS: a warrior driving a chariot; an armed soldier

GOD/DESS FORMS: Ares; Horus; Mars; Tiw

CREATURES: basilisk; bear; horse; she-goat; stag; wolf

DOMICILE: Aries; Scorpio

DETRIMENT: Libra; Taurus

EXALTATION: Capricorn

FALL: Cancer

GOD NAME: Elohim Gebur

ARCHANGEL: Samael

ANGEL: Seraphim

SPIRIT: Phaleg (Bartzabel)

INTELLIGENCE: Graphiel

SEPHIRA: Geburah (Severity)

TAROT CARD: the Tower (XVI)

FLOWERS: anemone; carnation; geranium; hollyhock; lupine; Siberian squill; yellow daffodil

INCENSE: benzoin; dragons blood; lodestone; mastic; patchouli; pepper; pine; santal; sulphur; tobacco.

PERFUMES: carnation; pine; scotch broom

PLANTS: absinthe; barberry; basil; betony; briar; broom; bryony; cactus; capers; coriander; cowslip; dragon's blood; flaxseed; garlic; gentian; ginger; hellebore; hops; horseradish; hyssop; lamb's tongue; leek; mustard; nettles; onions; pepper; plantain; rue; rush; sarsaparilla; tarragon; tragacanth

WOODS: box tree; cedar; cypress; dogwood; hawthorn; hemlock; pine; santal

TIME: prime of life

NEGATIVE EFFECTS ON PERSONALITY: hatred; rage; impatience

PARTS OF THE BODY: muscular system; sex organs; blood; motor nerves

TONE: C

LETTER: O

RITUAL THEMES: surgery; focusing energy; motivation; endurance; encouragement; dealing with contractors or builders; strength; athletic competition; discord; warfare; combat; the armed forces; victory; domination; lawsuits; protection

MERCURY

DAY: Wednesday

GENDER: androgynous

NUMBER: 8

DIRECTION: east

COLORS: yellow; orange; multi-colors; violet

GEMSTONES: agate; opal

METAL: quicksilver

GOD/DESS FORMS: Anubis; Hermes; Maat; Mercury; Odin; Pan; Thoth

CREATURES: baboon; bear; crane; dog; ibis; jackal; magpie; swallow; two snakes entwined

SYMBOL: a slim man with winged feet and cap; a staff with entwined serpents; cloak of concealment

DOMICILE: Gemini; Virgo

DETRIMENT: Sagittarius; Pisces

EXALTATION: Aquarius

FALL: Leo

GOD NAME: Elohim Tzabaoth

ARCHANGEL: Raphael

ANGEL: Benei Elohim

SPIRIT: Ophiel (Taphthar Tharath)

INTELLIGENCE: Tiriel

SEPHIRA: Hod (Glory)

TAROT CARD: the Magician (I)

FLOWERS: artificial flowers; azalea; jasmine; lavender; lilac; lily-of-the-valley; narcissus; sweet pea; violet

INCENSE: cinnamon; mace; mastic; orange peel; sandalwood; storax

PERFUMES: clover; mace; narcissus; sandalwood

PLANTS: anise; Brazil nut; calamint; caraway; carrots; cashews; calamint; cinquefoil; citron; dill; elecampane; fennel; fenugreek; filbert; hound's-tongue; horehound; lavender; licorice; linseed; maidenshair; mandrake; marjoram; oats; orris; parings from wood and fruit; parsley; parsnip; peyote; pomegranate; savory; southernwood; valerian; wild garlic

WOODS: cinnamon; hazel; mulberry; myrtle; sandalwood

TIME: early education

NEGATIVE EFFECTS ON PERSONALITY: lack of emotion; amorality; over-intellectualization; inability to focus thoughts; surface knowledge

PARTS OF THE BODY: brain; mouth; nervous system; pituitary; parathyroid; thyroid glands; pulmonary and respiratory circulation; vocal chords

TONE: B

LETTER: A

RITUAL THEMES: education; intellect; creativity; writing; literature; inspiration; studying; learning languages; communication; information gathering; commerce; sales; counseling; diplomacy; medicine; quick changes; adaptation for survival; tarot; divination; professional advancement; High Magic; travel safety; making purchases; theatrical performances; storm-raising; treatment of infertility and nervous disorders; taking responsibility for one's own actions

JUPITER

DAY: Thursday

GENDER: masculine

NUMBER: 4

DIRECTION: southeast

COLORS: sky blue; purple; indigo

GEMSTONES: amethyst; carnelian; lapis lazuli; sapphire; turquoise

METAL: tin

GOD/DESS FORMS: Amon; Dagda; Jupiter; Marduk; Poseidon; Thor; Zeus

CREATURES: bull; dragon; eagle; peacock; stag; unicorn

SYMBOL: crowned king; saffron robe; sword

DOMICILE: Sagittarius; Pisces

DETRIMENT: Gemini; Virgo

EXALTATION: Cancer

FALL: Aries

GOD NAME: El

ARCHANGEL: Sachiel

ANGEL: Chasmalim

SPIRIT: Bethor (Hesmael)

INTELLIGENCE: Iophiel

TAROT CARD: the Wheel of Fortune (X)

SEPHIRA: Chesed (Mercy)

FLOWERS: arnica; carnation; jasmine; lilac; narcissus; pinks; roses; stock

INCENSE: balsam; bay; benzoin; myrrh; storax

PERFUMES: balm; carnation; cedar; civet; jasmine; musk; narcissus; saffron; sage

PLANTS: agrimony; anise; asparagus; balm; balm of Gilead; bay; betony; black currant; borage; briar rose; cedar; chervil; chestnut; chicory; cinquefoil; clove; dandelion; datura; dock; evergreens; fruits of all trees; ginseng; grains of paradise; henbane; houseleek; hyssop; linden; liverwort; mint; mistletoe; mulberry; nutmeg; olives; orris root; queen-of-the-meadow; rosehips; saffron; sage; turnip; verbena; watercress

WOODS: almond; aloes; ash; balsam; birch; box tree; cedar; chestnut; cinnamon; fig; fir; maple; oak; pine; poplar; sumac

TIME: middle age

NEGATIVE EFFECTS ON PERSONALITY: extravagance; over-confidence; hedonism

PARTS OF THE BODY: adrenal glands; arteries; liver; pancreas

TONE: A

LETTER: E

RITUAL THEMES: higher education; career; philosophy; ambition; religion; justice; family; friendship; groups; opportunities; health; male infertility; prosperity; luck; hope; harmony; real estate; long-distance travel; expansion; the fields of medicine and sports; banking; debt collection; life changes

VENUS

DAY: Friday

GENDER: feminine

NUMBER: 7

DIRECTION: west

COLORS: green; yellow-green; blue-green; pink

GEMSTONES: carnelian; emerald; turquoise

METALS: bronze; copper

GOD/DESS FORMS: Aphrodite; Astarte; Brigit; Cordelia; Freya; Hathor; Morwyn; Venus

CREATURES: camel; cat; dove; leopard; lynx; she-goat; sparrow; swan

SYMBOL: a naked girl

DOMICILE: Taurus; Libra

DETRIMENT: Scorpio; Aries

EXALTATION: Pisces

FALL: Virgo

GOD NAME: Jehovah Tzabaoth

ARCHANGEL: Anael

ANGELS: Tarsishim; the Elohim

SPIRIT: Hagith (Kedemiel)

INTELLIGENCE: Hagiel

TAROT CARD: the Empress (III)

SEPHIRA: Netzach (Victory)

FLOWERS: apple blossom; bleeding heart; clover; columbine; daffodil; daisy; damask rose; foxglove; geranium; gladiolus; honeysuckle; mock orange; myrtle; pansy; peach blossom; primrose; rose; sweet pea

INCENSE: clove; jasmine; musk; sandalwood; vanilla

PERFUMES: ambergris; damask rose; honeysuckle; jasmine; musk; white rose; sandalwood; violet

PLANTS: angelica; apple; apricot; artichoke; blackberry; bramble; burdock; catnip; chestnut; cherry; chick-pea; clover; coltsfoot; cowslip; damiana; elderberry; fennel; fern; feverfew; figs; gooseberry; grape; ivy; lady's mantle; lady slipper lovage; maidenhair; marshmallow; mint; motherwort; mugwort; peach; pear; pennyroyal; pepperwort; plantain; raspberry; saffron; sorrel; spearmint; strawberry; tansy; thyme; tomato; verbena; vervain; violet; wheat; yarrow

WOODS: apple; black alder; birch; cherry; myrtle; sycamore

TIME: adolescence

NEGATIVE EFFECTS ON PERSONALITY: overindulgence; slothfulness; vanity; too much sensuality

PARTS OF THE BODY: cheeks; chin; gonads; hair; kidneys; skin; throat; thyroid glands; sense of touch; veins

TONE: E

LETTER: U

RITUAL THEMES: friendship; love; ecstasy; pleasure; sex; marriage; partnerships; harmony; fertility; beauty; the arts and crafts; music; creativity; literature; social affairs; rituals involving the animal or vegetable kingdoms; offspring; compassion

SATURN

DAY: Saturday

GENDER: masculine

NUMBER: 3

DIRECTION: north

COLORS: black; dark blue; gray; indigo

GEMSTONES: jet; onyx; sapphire

METAL: lead

GOD/DESS FORMS: Ceres; Ceridwen; Cybele; Danu; Demeter; Hecate; Kronos; Nephthys; Nut; Persephone; Rhea; Saturn

CREATURES: camel; crocodile; goat

SYMBOLS: old man or woman leaning on a staff; scythe

DOMICILE: Capricorn; Aquarius

DETRIMENT: Cancer; Leo

EXALTATION: Libra

FALL: Aries

GOD NAME: Jehovah Elohim

ARCHANGEL: Cassiel

ANGEL: Aralim

SPIRIT: Aratron; (Zazel)

INTELLIGENCE: Agiel

TAROT CARD: The World (XXI)

SEPHIRA: Binah

FLOWERS: black poppy; dried flowers; gladiolus; hyacinth; pansy; wallflowers

INCENSE: dittany of Crete; myrrh; pine; vetiver

PERFUMES: alum; civet; musk; myrrh

PLANTS: asafoetida; barley; boneset; buckthorn; century plant; cereals; coffee; comfrey; dried fruit; hay; hellebore; hemlock; henbane; knotgrass; mandrake; marijuana; monkshood; mullein; mushrooms; nightshade; oakmoss; parsnip; patchouli; pepperwort; plantain; quince; rhubarb; rushes; rye; shepherd's purse; Solomon's seal; sorrel; spinach; thyme; wintergreen

WOODS: ash; beech; blackthorn; cypress; elm; juniper; oak; pine; poplar; yew

TIME: old age

NEGATIVE EFFECTS ON PERSONALITY: depression; rigidity; intolerance; isolation; inhibition

PARTS OF THE BODY: hair; bones

TONE: G

LETTER: X

RITUAL THEMES: poverty; property; real estate; wills; elderly people; old plans; death; self-control; responsibility; dignity; doctrine; karma; psychic self-defense; exorcism; inner knowledge; study for examinations; endurance; finding objects that have been stolen; organization; teachers; authority figures; building; mining; self-improvement; karmic patterns

URANUS

DAY: Saturday

METAL (mineral): uranium

GOD/DESS FORM: the sky god/dess

COLORS: electric blue; dazzling white

SYMBOL: Star

NUMBER: 10

DOMICILE: Aquarius

DETRIMENT: Leo

EXALTATION: Scorpio
FALL: Taurus
ARCHANGEL: Uriel
TAROT CARD: the Hierophant; reversed
INCENSE: frankincense
PERFUMES: atractylis; curcuma; elemi; musk
Flowers: Scotch broom; clover; orange blossom
PLANTS: ambrette seed; coconut; oxalis; rue
WOODS: amber resin; ash; fir
TONE: astral chimes
LETTERS: I; J; and Y
NEGATIVE EFFECTS ON PERSONALITY: intractability; eccentricity; explosive anger; "too many irons in the fire"
PARTS OF THE BODY: eyes; pupils; nervous system; parathyroid
RITUAL THEMES: astrology; travel; independence; intuition; inventions; freedom; revolution; rituals involving electrical energy; anything of an unconventional or unusual nature

NEPTUNE

DAY: Friday
GOD/DESS FORMS: Morrighan; Neptune; Poseidon
COLORS: blue-green; iridescence; lavender
METALS: neptunium; platinum
DOMICILE: Pisces
DETRIMENT: Virgo
GEMSTONE: pearl
ARCHANGEL: Asariel
NUMBER: 11
CREATURE: horse
EXALTATION: Leo
FALL: Aquarius
PERFUMES: cypress; eucalyptus; fougere; syringa

PLANTS: ferns; narcotic plants; rushes; seaweed; water lilies

NEGATIVE EFFECTS ON PERSONALITY: psychosis; elusiveness; obsessiveness; impressionability; tendency to be "wishy-washy"

TONE: music of the spheres

LETTERS: C; K

PARTS OF THE BODY: parathyroid and pineal glands; penal canal; elimination of toxins

RITUAL THEMES: creativity; dreams; drugs; divination; photography; mystical experiences; rituals involving the sea; any kind of travel; or artifice

PLUTO

DAY: Tuesday

GOD/DESS FORMS: Hades; Kore

COLORS: black; ultraviolet

METAL: plutonium

DOMICILE: Scorpio

DETRIMENT: Taurus

EXALTATION: Aquarius

FALL: Leo

LETTER: T

ARCHANGEL: Azrael

SPIRIT: Choir of Angels

INCENSE: opoponax

PERFUMES: ambergris; ambrosia; labdanum; syringa

FLOWERS: begonia; stephanotis

PLANTS: datura; peat

NEGATIVE EFFECTS ON PERSONALITY: oppression; destruction tempered by mercy

PART OF THE BODY: the third eye

TONE: harmony

RITUAL THEMES: destruction; pest control; transformation; regeneration; sex magic; charisma; editing; inheritance; wealth; contacting the spirits of the dead; self-examination; risks

Planetary Rite of Mercury
To Learn to Communicate with Animals and to Find the Animal Spirit Within Oneself

As I cast around to find a suitable subject for a planetary ritual, I resolved not to explore the ordinary topics of love (Venus), prosperity (Jupiter, Sun), health (Sun, Mercury), or revenge (Mars, Saturn), of which much has been written. Instead, I opted for an unusual theme : understanding animals and working with the animal soul within yourself. For years I have been fascinated with animals and have loved and cared for them. And since Mercury governs this realm of knowledge and also rules my own Sun sign, I decided that this would make an appropriate challenge.

The idea of contacting the animal soul within is not new. The section that follows this ritual describes the close link that always has existed between human and animal worlds. Witches believe that each of us still retains deep within the subconscious mind a strong affinity with at least one animal, and that the particular characteristics of this creature, in part, compel us on a subliminal level. To contact, understand, and master this spirit promotes self understanding and magical self-development.

The following ritual requires elaborate preparations because in planetary rites particularly, you need to construct the proper atmosphere in order to effectively arouse your imagination and direct your will toward performing the rite successfully. As Patricia Crowther, renowned British High Priestess, reminds us "The purpose of any ritual is to produce within the participants a thrilling of their astral bodies, which should vibrate through the whole being, the words and actions strongly moving and stimulating the people involved."[20] To this end, colored lights, music, incense, candles and other paraphernalia combine to create an environment that helps the participant to experience the inner meaning of the planetary force, and to intensify concentration on the purpose of the ritual.

When you review the characteristics of Mercury listed above, you will recall that this sphere represents communication, eloquence, wit, understanding, wisdom, adeptness with foreign languages, adaptability, creativity, skillfulness, grace, expression through dance, the power to heal humans and animals, and to understand and communicate with animals. Be sure that all participants have a clear idea of these concepts before they attempt the rite.

The spirits of the sphere of Mercury which I choose to invoke are described in Franz Bardon's book, *The Practice of Magical Evocation* (Wuppertal, Germany: Dieter Rüggherz, 1975). They are: Omael—friend and healer of the animal kingdom; Manakel—the spirit who shows how to influence all animals; Nanael—the spirit who reveals how to control animals and understand their language and communicate with their physical and astral bodies.

Items Required

You will need a light masked with an orange filter to lend a soft orange glow to the ritual site. Another important mood-maker—and focus of the Crane Dance (an integral part of the ritual),—is the music you choose to play. I suggest something African with a persistent, sensual drum beat. You may wish to use a long-playing cassette so you don't have to pause to rewind it. I favor Brazilian music such as *Primal Roots* by Sergio Mendes or recordings of Macumba (Brazilian popular religion) ceremonies.

Other items necessary for the ritual include: two orange altar candles anointed with Mercury oil, lighted before the commencement of the ritual; a yellow altar cloth; a vase of lilacs for the altar; Merlin's Magic incense; burner, coal and matches; dried lavender and orange blossoms in a silver bowl as an offering to the spirits of Mercury; a deep lavender-colored "cloak of concealment," consisting of a curtain fitted across the back of the altar so that it can be pulled open easily; a black mirror on the wall behind the curtain; the symbol of Mercury (figure 11) drawn in silver on a violet background on a piece of cardboard and placed in front of the curtain; a circular cloth with an inscribed orange triangle and the spirit names, Onael, Manakel, and Nanael written in silver along the inside of the triangle laid on the ground in front of the altar; drums, maracas, flutes, and other noisemakers; a pot of strong Thoth tea, which combines one part licorice, one part citron or orange peel, 1/2 part elecampane, and a sprinkling of marjoram; sandalwood anointing oil; a hat cut from cardboard made to resemble that worn by Mercury (figure 12), covered with silver paper or spray-painted. (Make the hat large enough to fit everybody's head without drooping down over their eyes.) If possible, coveners should dress in orange, silver, or lavender robes.

Figure 11: Symbol of Mercury

The Rite

Before opening the Circle, the coveners drink Thoth tea and meditate on the purpose of the rite. At the appropriate moment, the Priestess, wearing the Mercury cap, opens the Circle using the Lesser Banishing and Invoking Pentagram rituals. She anoints each participant on the third eye with sandalwood oil and invokes Hermes.

INVOCATION TO HERMES
Priestess: "Lord of eloquence, wit and wisdom, you who are known to us as Hermes, Thoth, Odin, and Pan, our Circle of Light poises expectantly on the brink of understanding."

All: "Hermes! Thoth! Odin! Pan!"

Priestess: "Crane-Watcher from the Inner Planes, step lightly into our minds, and reveal to us the silver strands that connect us with the kingdom of animals."

All: "Hermes! Thoth! Odin! Pan!"

Priestess: "I invoke you to swoop down upon our Circle and lift your great wings to reveal to us the way to understand and communicate with animal souls."

All: "Hermes! Thoth! Odin! Pan!
We seek to understand!
Pan! Odin! Hermes! Thoth!
Raise our animal souls aloft!

Figure 12: Helmet of Mercury

So that we may know within our hearts
The beast soul of which we form a part!"

INVOCATION OF THE SPIRITS OF MERCURY

As the Priest steps forward to the altar, the Priestess places the Mercury cap on his head and retires. He kneels and raises aloft the bowl of dried lavender petals and orange blossoms.

Priest: "Spirits of the quick-silver sphere, Omael, Manakel, Nanael, I invoke you to enter our Circle of Light and reveal to us the way to obtain the power of communication with the animal kingdom. As a token of our good faith and thanks to you for sharing these secrets, we offer you this bowl of fragrant lavender and orange flowers, symbols of the perfumed vibrations of your shimmering world."

The Priest replaces the bowl on the altar, goes to the East, and draws the Aquarius sign (figure 13) in the air with his invoking wand.

Priest: "Symbol of Humanity, let us be reminded that we, too are animals."

The Priest moves to the South and traces the Leo symbol, saying: "Lion of Fire, we entreat you to make us courageous in this endeavor."

In the West, the Priest inscribes the Scorpio sign and says: "Eagle who soars above, inspire us in our undertaking."

At the Northern Quarter, the Priest outlines a Taurus sign, saying: "Indefatigable, laborious Ox, instill us with the virtues of industriousness and patience so that we may ever strive to succeed in our efforts."

Figure 13: Symbol of Aquarius

Now the Priest goes to the center of the Circle, where he stands in front of the inscribed circle and triangle, lifts his left hand above his head pointed to the heavens, and points down to the center of the triangle with his wand (which should virtually vibrate in his hand).

Priest: "Omael, Manakel, Nanael, we summon you to manifest on this plane of existence. Come to us here and now. Hear and appear!

All (concentrating on the circle and triangle):

"Omael, Manakel, Nanael!

Omael, Manakel, Nanael!

Omael, Manakel, Nanael!

Omael, Manakel, Nanael!

Omael, Manakel, Nanael!

Omael, Manakel, Nanael!

Omael, Manakel, Nanael!
Manifest, Manifest, Manifest!
Manifest, Manifest, Manifest!
MANIFEST!"

The Priest pauses for a few moments poised in the above-described posture, while everyone concentrates on manifesting the Spirits of Mercury. When the Priestess rings the bell, the Priest gives her the cap, and returns to the edge of the Circle.

CRANE DANCE

Priestess (with cap on head): "Now we shall perform the crane dance, the purpose of which is to contact our animal souls. To put us in the right mood and rhythm, we will begin by listening for awhile to the music. Then I will lead the dance that will spiral from the center of the Circle to the East, South, North, West, and East again in a figure-eight configuration. When I feel the spirit come to me, I will stop and kneel by the altar and remove the symbol of Mercury from in front of the cloak of concealment. At that moment, everyone will go to the edge of the Circle, pick up, and begin to play a musical instrument marking time to the music. If you cannot play an instrument, clap your hands.

"Then I will draw back the cloak of concealment and contemplate the image that appears to me. When I am finished, I will close the curtain, remove the hat, place it on the altar, resume my place at the edge of the Circle, and begin to play an instrument.

"Next, anyone who feels the spirit should rise, don the hat, and dance the figure-eight pattern until she or he feels ready to draw back the cloak. All the while the rest of the group marks time with the drums and rattles. We will proceed in this way until each of us has had a chance to discover the animal spirit waiting behind the cloak of concealment."

The Priestess starts the music and proceeds according to plan. When the dance is over, those who wish to do so may share their experiences with the group. The Priestess closes the Circle with the Lesser Banishing Pentagram Ritual and gives the spirits license to depart. The rite is ended.

Be sure to have plenty of liquid refreshment and finger-food available for after the ritual, as participants are likely to be thirsty and hungry after their exertions.

The Significance of Animals

The relationship between humans and animals is complex. From earliest times we have relied on animals as a source of food, transportation, and even clothing and weapons. Many animals remain faithful friends and companions while others are viewed with fear and awe for their superior physical and sensory prowess. Most, in one way or another, have earned our respect.

In primitive times, many creatures were especially admired for their superior strength and abilities to ferret out, run down, and dispatch their prey, which often included humans. In those days the line between human beings and animals was less distinct than it is today. People believed that by dressing in rival beasts' hides, performing their dances, and eating their flesh, they would be endowed with the creatures' superior qualities.

Some cultures believed (and still do today) that animals sense more than we do about the environment, and that portents of good, evil, prosperity, and disaster can be foretold by studying their movements and voices. Some societies even attempted to read auguries in their entrails. Even today, I have encountered many people—especially farmers who otherwise might shun any connection with the occult—who attempt to predict the weather by observing when birds fly, how heavy wild creatures' coats grow, when squirrels start to hide nuts, etc.

In some cultures, veneration for animals evolved into worship. For example, the ancient Egyptians envisioned part-human, part-animal gods. They numbered a variety of animals and quasi-animals in their pantheon, including the cow, crane, hippopotamus, cat, bull, ibis, snake, jackal, and crocodile. Their animal-human gods are divided into three categories: theriomorphic (animal forms), anthropomorphic (human form), therianthropic (hybrid form with human body and animal head).

Throughout Europe tales of half-feral, half-human entities such as the horned Cernunnos, the Minotaur, and the Mermaid show the deep-rooted belief in animals as gods, and the merging of human and animal forms. Many tribes affiliated themselves with one particular animal, who then became the totem of the group. This custom persisted with the native North American Indians, and today forms an integral part of many Native American Shamanistic traditions.

Witches always have been believed to keep animals as familiars. In fact, during the Witch hunt hysteria, to have a special pet could implicate a person in the practice of Witchcraft. At that time, a familiar was defined as a discarnate human, a non-human spirit, elemental, or an actual animal that attended the sorcerer or sorceress, and helped perform magic and spirit communication. Witches were accused of feeding these animals their own blood or milk to establish and maintain a psychic connection with them.

These stories probably originated because of animals' superior abilities to sense danger and also their strong reactions to corpses and haunted places. Cats and dogs always have been especially adept at these kinds of "sixth sense" perceptions. Witches, who generally lived closer to the natural world than others, recognized their pets' abilities and relied on them to help protect themselves, heal others, predict changes in weather, identify hauntings, etc. Many Christians of the Witch hunt era felt threatened by animals' special skills that they did not understand, and so reacted swiftly and barbarously by burning, drowning, or strangling the animals and their caretakers. In so doing, they reaffirmed their own bestial ancestry.

This is not to say, however, that all Witches and Magicians have always maintained pure intentions toward the animal kingdom in their rituals. Some sects incorporate or have incorporated animal sacrifices into their rituals. Originally, people hunted, killed, and ate animals whose prowess they coveted in an attempt to assimilate these abilities. As humans gained more control over animals, they used their power of life and death over these creatures to utilize their life forces and direct them into rituals to add strength and energy to their rites. Such practices still occur in some forms of Voodun and Brazilian religions.

The Wicca tradition, of which our group is a part, does not believe that animal sacrifice is justified. We hold that since we are animals ourselves, we are no better or worse than any other animal, and have no right to use the life force of any living being to our own ends. While we admit we need to kill animals and plants in order to survive (or more likely, pick them canned, frozen, or wrapped off the grocery store shelves), we do so because continuance of our species is instinctual and necessary. However, we believe that to kill animals for magical purposes is not necessary to our lives. We prefer to use other methods to raise cones of power, such as those described in this and other of books on Witchcraft. We do not condemn those of highly respected traditions such as Voodun and Macumba who use animal life forces in this way, nor do we deny the indisputable effectiveness of such practices in relieving human suffering. Nevertheless, we do not choose that path for ourselves.

An Occult Bestiary

A bestiary is a collection of moral tales about animals that may be real or fictitious. Bestiaries achieved high popularity in medieval Christian Europe, and are still studied for their valuable insights into the meanings of Christian animal symbolism.

The following occult bestiary is an abbreviated list of some of the real animals most frequently encountered in occult symbolism. It describes animals and some of the myths and characteristics that have come to be connected with them. I include only real animals because the purpose of the bestiary is to act as a point of departure to help give you the idea for finding the spirit animal that dwells within you for your Mercury rite.

BAT

These flying mammals probably earned their evil reputation because of their wicked appearance, nocturnal habits, and secretive living environment (hidden away in caves, barns, and attics). The Irish identify bats with death; Middle Europeans associate bats with vampires (indeed, blood-drinking vampire bats exist); Nigerians believe that bats can enter the body and need to be routed out by an expert exorcist.

Not all cultures think bats are evil. Some American Indian tribes include this flying mammal among their totems as a symbol of rebirth and introspection. Indians revere their rapid, almost soundless flight, nocturnal visual acumen, and ability to see at night and zero in on their prey. In China, the animal represents long life and happiness. Among those who practice Voodun worldwide, bat blood is added to potions to unite lovers, bring good luck to gamblers, and vanquish enemies.

A completely different symbolism of the bat that has persisted throughout myth is its role as protector of humans. Perhaps this derives from its large wing span, which may be construed as a protective mantle, or from its nighttime activity; hence, bats are thought to be night watchers. This chivalrous association has been portrayed in recent times by the popular Batman comic character.

BEAR

The bear was considered a powerful totem among many primitive tribes and shamanistic religions such as those of the American Indians, Estonians, Finns, Lapps, Lithuanians, and Russians. Its immense strength and ability to walk upright led humans to see in it an affinity with the supernatural. To the American Indians, the creature's habit of hibernating in winter suggested an association with introspection and female receptivity. Many ancient people believed bears really were gods. So they killed them ceremonially and ate their flesh in order to assimilate the god's powers. A well researched and entertaining novel that describes the fascination of bears for primitive people is Jean Auel's *Clan of the Cave Bear*. [21]

On another level, psychologists identify the bear with our most deep-rooted fears. Perhaps this is why for Alchemists, the bear represented prime matter and instinct. Bears also are associated with cruelty and crudeness.

BIRDS

Perhaps because of their ability to soar to the heavens, and the fact that the cries of some species sound uncannily like human speech, many species of birds have been credited with magical powers. Their movements, calls, colors, and habits also have been studied as sources of augury in many cultures.

DOVE

A renowned symbol of love, peace, and the Holy Spirit, doves also harbinger sadness and mourning. Probably they acquired their reputation as love and fertility birds from their prolific breeding habits. Greeks and Romans sacrificed doves to the goddess of love, Aphrodite. In depictions of Aphrodite, she travels across the sky in a chariot drawn by doves. In the Bible, Noah sends a dove to see if the flood waters have receded. The bird returns with an olive branch in its beak, an image which has come to represent tranquility, prosperity, and peace. As a symbol of world peace doves are still released into the air at the modern Olympiads.

The voices of doves are used in divination, and a white dove symbolizes purity. Some Slavs believe that at the point of death a person's soul transforms into this bird.

CRANE

The Chinese associate the crane with a long life and a just and diligent soul. Other cultures liken it to the Sun in its aspect as harbinger of spring. The crane is also associated with Hermes, communicator and messenger of the gods. In Crete, the crane dance, which simulates the labyrinth-like mating dance of the bird, is still performed for fertility.

EAGLE

The flight path of an eagle—a grand, majestic spiral toward the Sun—is an awe-inspiring sight that connects this bird to the concepts of air, fire, spirit, imagination, opportunity, prayer, divine majesty thunderbolts, and sky powers. The sky potencies are also fertilizing powers, and cultures as varied as the Mexican Aztecs, American Hopi Indians, Arabs, and Qabalistic Magicians related this noble bird to water, fertility, and procreation. Alchemists use the symbol of the eagle to stand for volatilization. The Egyptian hieroglyph for the letter A is an eagle, which stands for the warmth of light, origin, and daylight. The East Indian garuda, a body of a man with the head and wings of an eagle, symbolizes the wind. In Imperial Rome and in the United States, the bird is an emblem of power. It also accompanies Zeus/Jupiter as a stormbird, symbol of the power of thunder. The eagle also is identified with the astrological sign, Aquarius, and thus, stands for all that is high-minded and spiritual.

RAVEN

The raven is an oracular bird associated with High Magic. Odin carried two ravens on his shoulders, whom he sent through the world to bring back the news of the day. The Celtic war goddesses, Fea, Badb, Nemon, and Macha appeared to the tribes as ravens in the heat of battle. The Scots call the raven the Bird of Truth, and some Cornish people will not kill ravens because they believe that when King Arthur died, he was transformed into this bird. By custom in England, ravens are kept perpetually at the Tower of London because it is believed that if they ever leave, England will fall under foreign domination. Other cultures focus on the raven's black plumage and habit of eating carrion, and associate the bird with death, squalor, the devil, and consequently, with Witchcraft. The Egyptians looked beyond this superficiality to deify the raven as a powerful symbol of Mother Nature in her aspect as ruler over death and transformation. To the American Indians the bird signifies the unknown and the healing power of magic.

CAT

Throughout recorded time, and in accordance with the attitudes expressed by various cultures, the fortunes of the cat have waxed and waned like the Moon. In ancient Egypt, the cat was worshipped in the form of the goddess, Bast, an aspect of Isis. An entire city was built to honor cats, and when a cat died, its owner would shave its eyebrows and go into mourning. To kill a cat was punishable by death. Cats were also connected with the goddesses Diana and Freyja, and enjoyed a reputation as seers—probably due to the clear beauty of their eyes and their inscrutable behavior.

With the rise of Christianity cats fell from grace along with all things Pagan. They were linked with Witches and accused of being their familiars, or even actual Witches in disguise. For this reason they were burned at the stake as malefactors. In England, sacks of live cats were thrown onto fires on Guy Fawkes Day. The English also burned cats on Easter Sunday and Shrove Thursday in an attempt to rid villages of evil influences. Cats were killed if they dared venture near corpses for fear of their stealing the souls of the dead. Even today, many people keep cats away from babies' cribs because they think they will smother the infants.

In spite of the imprecations of "felinophobics," there are those who love and cherish these loyal but independent, cuddly but proud, engaging little creatures and welcome them into their homes.

Cow

In Egypt, cows were worshipped as a sign of fertility, life, and nourishment. These characteristics were embodied in the cow-headed goddess, Hathor, who was revered as the manifestation of the divine bounty of the earth. In India it is thought that when people die, the zebu cows will guide their souls to the other world; thus cows are known as the Pathfinders.

Dog

Many cultures over time have thought of dogs as the consummate guardian animals, and by extension, the conductors of souls to the afterlife. Therefore, dogs are deified in figures like Anubis (Egypt) and Cerberus (Greece). Statues of guard dogs flank the entrances to temples in Tibet and China. Dog ghosts were believed to lead their masters to hidden treasures. The dog as hunter is remembered as the companion of Artemis/Diana in her wanderings in the forest.

Esteemed today for their loyalty, dogs hold a place of honor in many homes, particularly those of the British. The Hindus so believed in canine powers that they considered them equal to humans, and consequently, tried them in courts like humans, and had them punished or killed if they bit anybody. In Alchemy the symbol of the dog devoured by the wolf represents purification of gold by antimony.

DOLPHIN

Stories about dolphins are popular these days. More and more scientific research is being carried out as to their intelligence and communicative abilities. Tales abound that cite how amicable dolphins are with people, and how they have rescued humans from sharks and drowning. Legend has it that once these mammals lived on land, but disgusted with how it was being mismanaged by humans, they retreated to the sea. Dolphin associations include: salvation (friend of humans); divine wisdom and love (it is the animal of Apollo, Aphrodite and Eros); swiftness, prudence, life, and death (they are said to transport the gods to their resting places); the cosmic stream of involution and evolution (symbolized by two arrows meeting and passing in opposite directions); and the life force.

HORSE

The conquerors of Mexico recorded that the Aztecs thought that the horses the Spaniards had brought with them were superhuman beasts that would ravage the countryside. Swifter than the fastest human, their thunderous hooves raising a deafening racket , these huge, sweating, hulks struck terror into the hearts of the Indians. For a long time the natives believed that horses were immortal.

In Britain, gigantic figures of horses have been discovered cut into the white chalk of the countryside. The most famous is the white horse of Uffington in Berkshire. It may be that these immense figures were used in fertility rites long ago. (As an outgrowth of this theme, in tea-leaf reading a horse's head is symbolic of the appearance of a lover.) In other cultures, muscular stallions were depicted as pulling the chariot of the sun across the sky. The horse, representation of strength, speed, grace, and fertility, has remained a potent symbol throughout the ages.

SNAKE

Because it was the tempter in the Garden of Eden, the serpent ever since has received bad press, and has come to be known as the symbol of evil incarnate. However, not all cultures have perceived the snake as the representation of the Devil. This cold-blooded creature also stands for fertility, immortality, pure energy, wisdom, and spiritual riches. In India, a snake cult connects the serpent with the water of the sea, and hails it as the guardian of the spring of life. Because of its ability to shed its skin and outwardly regenerate itself, it has become a symbol of transmutation and immortality. This representation is seen in the familiar Gnostic ourobouros, where the snake forms a circle, holding its tail in its mouth. Half of the depiction is dark, the other half is light, representing passion, negativity and destruction on one hand, activity, positivity, and construction on the other.

The serpent's ability to strangle its victims associates it with the principle of strength, and its threatening hissing noise and vicious mode of attack is akin to the abnormal stirrings of the unconscious mind. All in all, the serpent is a powerful totem. In Chinese astrology, the only animal capable of destroying the serpent is the boar.

Chapter Four
Sabbat Rites

In chapter 2 you learned about the Esbat rites that celebrate the Moon's monthly cycle. Lunar rites often tap into feminine energy. They usually involve themes such as personal and psychic self-development, spells, enchantments, or rituals geared to a specific purpose. Witches use the lunar tides to hold classes in which they strive to learn more about the Craft. Esbats often are closed to the uninitiated because they are viewed as workshops where Witches concentrate on using their occult power to perform Magic.

In contrast to the workshop atmosphere of the lunar rites, Sabbat rituals are celebratory. By performing these rites, Witches observe the cycle of life on earth as it is expressed in nature. Witches envision the Great Sabbats (there are eight of them, occurring at about six-week intervals) as taking place at certain positions on the Great Wheel of the Year. As the wheel turns, so the seasons come round—spring, summer, fall, winter, and spring again—in a never-ending circle of birth, death, and rebirth. Since the seasons are associated with the Sun, and the Sun is conceived of as masculine, the primary symbol emphasized is the male Child of Promise, who is also called the Child of Light. He is a Christ-like or Horus-like figure who moves through roughly three stages, as does the goddess. At the Winter Solstice, he is the Magical Child of

Light, born unto this world to save humanity with his procreative capacity.

In the spring and summer, he matures into the lusty Pagan god who enchants and then beds the goddess, impregnating her with the seed of life. He also embodies the aspect of the terrible, mighty, vengeful god, who is capable of crushing all else underfoot.

At the end of the year, his power spent and his virility withered, he dies. However, the goddess miraculously gives birth to him again at the Winter Solstice, and the cycle of life begins anew.

This myth parallels the evolution of the seasons of the year. Undoubtedly, many of the rites that follow will seem familiar to Christians, who similarly celebrate the birth of Christ, his death, and rebirth. This is because the Christian Church borrowed many elements from pre-Christian worship to make their religion appeal more to Pagans.

At the end of this chapter you will find a Sabbat Planner that summarizes these seasonal rituals. Use it as a reference to help you devise your own rites.

Winter Solstice—Alban Arthan
(December 19—22)

Witches welcome the New Year at the Winter Solstice when we celebrate the birth of the Child of Promise, symbol of our highest hopes and aspirations. At this intimate Sabbat coven members join together as a family in the privacy of the home. There we drink hot, spiced, mulled wine or cider, and exchange gifts for magical and psychic development.

Coveners often present mumming plays, which are a type of Christmas performance of British Christian origin, with Pagan roots. In a mumming play, St. George, the symbol of Light, battles a Turkish knight, symbol of Darkness. When at last he slays the foe, St. George cries out, "I have killed my brother!" For without darkness, there can be no light. Suddenly a mysterious doctor appears—probably a Christianized version of the Magician—and miraculously revives the knight with a potion. Everyone rejoices.

If possible, coveners burn a Yule log decorated with pine cones, holly, ribbons, bayberry leaves, and other signs of the season. As a reaffirmation of regeneration, coveners save part of the burned log to kindle the next year's Yule blaze. Supposedly the ashes from the log contain healing properties. When filtered through a piece of muslin and drunk, they reputedly cure diseases and grant wishes. Ashes scattered on cultivated ground increase its fertility.

Preparations

This ritual requires you to burn a Yule log. If you do not have a fireplace, substitute a cauldron with a mini-log or needfire mix. Place the altar, covered with a white or silver cloth, in the North. Festoon it with holly and pine cones to represent each coven member. Erect a small live Christmas tree on the altar. During the Yuletide season it is easy to obtain these trees at drugstores, grocery stores, or department and discount stores. Ideally, you should light the tree with miniature Christmas lights, but if these are not within your budget, or an electrical outlet is not handy, decorate the tree with imitation silver icicles so that it sparkles. Use the black candle from Hallowmas to open the Circle. Have empty candleholders ready on the altar, one for each covener, present or absent. Bear in mind that this is the most intimate Sabbat, the one where bonding takes place among members to strengthen the coven for the New Year. Celtic harp music creates a relaxing mood. Make incense from frankincense, myrrh pieces, benzoin powder, and mistletoe and pine oils. The Priestess anoints the coveners with fir oil before opening the Circle and places an acorn on the altar as a symbol of the resurrected god.

Each covener brings a white taper anointed with mistletoe oil, and a gift to exchange during the feast. In our coven we write each person's name on pieces of paper at Hallowmas, and draw names from a hat. We keep our selections secret until we exchange gifts. Everyone also brings decorations for the tree and hangs them before the ceremony begins. In addition, each person brings something with which to dress the Yule log, such as colored ribbons, pine cones, colorful pieces of cloth, sprigs of holly and mistletoe, etc., all of which are traditional embellishments. People bring evergreen boughs to ring the Circle, white robes to wear, and personal "soul trees" for naming during the rite. A soul tree is a small live tree that you name, water, and nourish, to which you can unburden your problems and from which you can receive strength and peace of mind in return. In this sense, the soul tree is a true friend (see chapter 6 for a detailed discussion of soul trees). In the spring, plant the tree outdoors in garden or forest. However, if these options are not convenient or available, choose an indoor tree such as a Norfolk pine or a palm. Such trees can change residence with you. Each covener writes the tree's name on a piece of parchment, perforates the paper with a small hole, and threads it with a piece of red yarn. During the rite, you will tie the parchment to the tree with the yarn.

Opening the Circle

As the ritual begins, the Circle is dark except for the light emitted by the Christmas tree and the candle in the South. Robed coveners holding soul trees, evergreen boughs, and candles form a line outside the Circle in the northeast Quadrant, behind the Priestess and Priest.

The Priestess lights the black candle and the coveners follow her into the Circle, circumnambulating it three times, then placing their soul trees in the center of the Circle and the evergreen boughs around the circumference. They take their places.

Priestess: "Winter Solstice is upon us and the shadows of the long winter nights imperceptibly begin to recede. With the return of the light to our cold and cheerless earth, the New Year dawns, brimming with life and hope, ideas and promises. As in days of old, let us celebrate the renewal of life."

The Priestess anoints each covener on the forehead with pine or spruce oil, then opens the Circle using the Greater Pentagram Ritual.

The Officers of the Quarters invoke the powers of the elements using the formulas described in chapter 1, or in any appropriate manner.

INVOCATION OF THE GODDESS

Priestess: "Mother goddess, whose image is reflected in the silver fir, enfold us in your shimmering branches, and weave a thatch of fragrance about us to protect us from the frost-bitter winds. We appeal to you to be present with us in our ritual. Your star-dusted branches reach out to us as a beam to guide us to the light."

INVOCATION OF THE GOD

Priest: "The Child of Promise of our souls' as yet unfulfilled dreams is born today. You who are known to us as Horus, Balder, and Christ, appear before us tonight, and fill our world with the vitality and ecstasy of your dance. We honor you tonight; for you bring us the gifts of life, love, and hope for the future!"

The Rite

Priestess: "The gift of life renewed is bestowed upon us by the Lord of Light. Since this is the season for giving, let us turn our thoughts to what we can donate of ourselves physically, psychically, and spiritually in the year to come. As we light our candles to help guide back the Sun to our sphere, let each of us affirm a gift to give in the New Year."

The Priestess lights the white candles from the black one, one for herself and one for each covener unable to attend the rite, and affirms her offering aloud. All follow suit, lighting their candles and making their offerings. This gift can be any sort of pledge, from a contribution to animal welfare to a promise to donate free massages to the coven, or a vow to light candles at each Full Moon for world peace.

When all the candles are lit, the Priest comes forward, extinguishes the black candle and pronounces:

"The old year is behind us. The new year is dawning. Let no one reflect on the old year with regret. Remember that the lessons learned from experience make us wise and form our history. Nothing is forgotten. I hereby declare the new year born!"

All: "Harahaya!"

The Priest lights the Yule log; the Priestess explains:

"Now we shall baptize our soul trees — personal friends from the kingdom of plants—who will guide us through the joys and sorrows of this year, lending us their support. In return we will nourish them and help them grow."

Beginning with the Priestess, each covener takes a piece of parchment with the tree's personal name written on it, and fastens the paper to the tree. Then she declares the tree's name aloud, saying for example, "I name you 'Dancing Wood,'" or "Henceforth you are known to me as 'Druid's Song'. By that name you are known to me, and so we are bound together in mutual friendship and respect." The covener sprinkles consecrated water around the dirt in which the tree is planted while reciting the name. One at a time, each person comes forward and performs the baptism procedure. When the naming ceremony is over, the Priest rises and says, "Let us together weave the dance of life and light, the dance of the yule wheel."

The Priest or Priestess changes the music to something more lively. Coveners join hands and wind around the soul trees dancing slowly at first, then faster and faster. When the dance reaches its climax, they let go of hands and direct energy into the soul trees, instilling them with love and the infinite capacity for growth. The group remains seated for a few minutes in quiet contemplation, revitalizing their personal life forces and cleansing their physical, mental, and spiritual auras.

Closing the Circle

The Priestess stands facing the altar and recites:

"If it is within the plan of the Divine Will, may the most secret dreams and goals of each and every one of us present here tonight be fulfilled within the next turn of the Great Wheel. So mote it be!"

The Priestess closes the Circle with the Lesser Banishing Pentagram Ritual and gives all spirits license to depart to their realms. The rite is ended. Feast and be merry!

As the coveners leave the Circle, they take away with them their white tapers to burn at the next Full Moon to help fulfill their desires. Also take a pine cone, a sprig of holly, and a cooled ember from the Yule log (or needfire). Wrap these items in a white silk cloth and place them under your pillow before retiring. You will receive a message from your Holy Guardian Angel (Higher Self) in a dream during the night.

Candlemas or Oilmec or Imbolg
(February 1)
Edited invocations by Rimaal; ritual by Morwyn

The Gaelic word for Candlemas is "Imbolg," which means "in the belly." The term is appropriate, for it connotes the waxing light of the Sun, still almost imperceptible, but gaining strength and substance daily, like a fetus in the womb. Besides celebrating the waxing light, Candlemas honors the fertility of the goddess. This is why during this ritual we fashion fire wheels, or swastikas, known as Brigit's crosses, and symbolically lay them in a bed to be fertilized by the god. In mythology, this is the time when Persephone, the goddess who was captured by Hades and forced to spend part of the year in the Underworld, reappears on Earth as the Springtime Maiden, whom we also call Kore, Morwyn, or Brigit. Because she spends part of her life in the realm of the unknown, Persephone personifies all three aspects of the goddess—maiden, mother, and hag. During the rite we appeal to her to reveal to us our hidden natures and talents, and to indicate the way to proceed on the Path. Besides the Fall Equinox, this is the most auspicious time for initiations.

Preparations

Use a brightly colored altar cloth in orange, red, or gold, embroidered or appliqued with fire tattvas. Festoon the altar with yellow daisies, chrysanthemums, and marigolds. Place eight gold candles at the Quarters and Cross-Quarters to represent the eight Great Sabbats, and flank the sides of the altar with orange or gold candles. Anoint these candles with Kore oil. Also place three black candles dressed with Persephone oil on the altar to represent the three aspects of the goddess. Ring the Circle with vervain for protection. Prepare Persephone incense from frankincense, myrrh, oakmoss, crushed juniper berries, and narcissus oil.

Coveners don bright robes and bring the following items to the Circle: a red candle and candleholder, straw to make the Brigit's crosses, and a small basket filled with batting, covered by an orange cloth for the bed in which the fire wheel will be fertilized. It is less costly if one person purchases a length of cloth and batting, and the coveners wait until they arrive at the ritual site to cut what they need to cover the bed.

Brigit's Crosses are fire wheels or swastikas made from straw. During the ceremony each covener takes handfuls of straw and shapes them into a swastika (fire wheel). To maintain the form, you need to mold the straw around two pipe cleaners that you bend into the swastika shape. Twist together the straw-covered pipe cleaners to make the fire wheel. Reinforce the form with red thread. Finally, lay the fire wheel into a small basket filled with batting or Easter grass, and cover the batting with a red or orange cloth to make the basket look like a mattress.

Opening the Temple

The Priestess enters the Circle from the Northeast, followed by the Priest and coveners. As the group takes their places, she lights the altar candles and eight Sabbat candles. She casts the Circle by any of the methods described in chapter 1 of this book. The Officers of the Quarters invoke the protection of the Archangels.

INVOCATION OF THE QUARTERS

East: "My mind touches your mind—*noscere*. Paralda, unleash your winds and send Raphael to us to guard this time, this place, and to protect all who are with us from that which is negative and unbalanced. Protector, let me be the current of your power."

South: "My passion arouses you—*velle*. Djinn, will the fires that shield your world to part so that Michael may charge forward to us. Michael, guard this time, this place, and all who are with us from that which is negative and unbalanced. Protector, let me be the vehicle of your power."

West: "In my unconscious you dare me to bring forth images from the deep well of my mind—*audere*. Nicksa, open the dam to the great unconsciousness so that Gabriel may stream forth to us to guard this time, this place, and all who are with us from that which is negative and unbalanced. Protector, let me be the vessel from which your power flows."

North: "My strength is in my silence—*tacere.* As Ghob holds apart the Earth, I use my strength to draw you forth. Auriel, guard this time, this place, and all who are with us from that which is negative and unbalanced. Protector, let me be the manifestation of your power."

The Priestess rings a bell: *"Noscere, velle, audere, tacere!* Welcome Great Guardians to our Circle of Light. In the name of all who dwell deep within your realms, I proclaim that the hour of the Sun's return is nigh. *Aerii, igneii, aquae, terrae spiriti, salvete!"*

The Rite

The coveners rise and go to the altar one by one, light a red taper and place it on the altar, saying something like "Sun, I welcome your return," "Evoe Persephone," "The Lord of Fire is among us."

Priestess: "The Wheel of the Year has turned, and we find ourselves facing the northeast Quarter of the Universe, celebrating Candlemas, the Feast of the Waxing Light. The light of the Sun increases and quickens the life that is locked in the drowsy, icebound earth."

INVOCATION OF PERSEPHONE

Priestess: "Tonight Persephone begins her journey up from the Underworld. As we invoke her to come into our presence, I want you to look deeply into the candle flames" —she lights candles—"one for the Virgin, one for the Mother, one for the Hag—therein lies the mystery of the three-form goddess. As I speak, I wish you to and meditate on what you need to fulfill your most secret desires and awaken your highest natures and talents.

"Tonight, Persephone, you shed your heavy cloak that no longer gives you warmth, and leave your black and barren world to be reborn as the springtime maiden. Clothed in bright and fragrant flowers, bathed in rippling candlelight, you materialize before us in our frost-bound world. Persephone, you who are known to us as Brigit, Kore, and Morwyn, be with us tonight! Bring us signs of spring and share with us your wisdom hard-won in the ghost-ridden world below. Illumine our paths!"

RITE OF BRIGIT'S CROSS
The coveners spend a few minutes in meditation. At the sound of the Priestess's bell, they are aroused from their reverie and bring to the center of the Circle straw and binding (thread, string, or ribbon), to make the Brigit's crosses.

Priestess: "We forge the Wheel of Brigit's Fire, and with it weave our cherished desires and latent powers. Then we lay our dreams to rest in beds brimming with the passion of our minds. We direct the power of the god force to manifest so that our desires may be brought to fruition."

The coveners lay the crosses in the prepared beds and move them into the center of the Circle.

INVOCATION TO THE GOD
As the Priest invokes the god, the coveners join hands and chant the god names Lugh, Helios, Baal, Thor, Ra (or other appropriate substitutes), softly at first, then louder and louder. After invoking, the Priest joins hands with the rest of the group. When the chant reaches its climax, they let go of hands and direct the energy they have invoked into the crosses.

Priest: "Lord of Fire, soaring with the eagles of the night, flaming passion, power beyond belief, you who compel us into the dance of life, I invoke you to spark our Circle with your might, and dance the dance of life with us tonight!"

Closing the Temple
After a few minutes of meditation the Priestess rises to close the Circle, thanks the spirits for their attendance at the rite, and gives them license to depart. Then she declares:

"*Noscere, velle, audere, tacere.* To know, to will, to dare, to keep silent! These are commands of Wicca, and by these laws we abide. *Aerii, ignei, aquae, terrae spiriti, valete!* Spirits of air, fire, water, and earth, we bid you farewell!"

The rite is ended. Feast and be merry! Take home your Brigit's cross and red candle, and burn the candle at the next Full Moon during a private rite, when you reaffirm your desires.

Spring Equinox/Vernal Equinox/Alban Eilir/ Festival of the Trees
(March 19—22)

With the Spring Equinox, or Festival of the Trees, arrives the true spring, when we honor the green-clad maiden and the laughing forest god. The Druidic month of Fearn means, "I am the shining tear of the Sun." This meaning reflects the union of fire and water, the combination of which fertilizes the earth. It is the planting season, so our coven ritually plants and waters seeds as representations of our highest aspirations. If weather permits, we also plant outdoors the live potted Yule tree from the Winter Solstice. The egg we eat during the ritual is a symbol of fertility of body, mind, and spirit. If a female covener wishes to become pregnant, she climbs a hill at the Spring Equinox, lights a needfire, and jumps over the cauldron.

The Spring Equinox is the true Mothers' Day, when Wicca mothers and daughters exchange cards and gifts and have dinners for each other in mutual appreciation. This custom is still observed at its proper time in Great Britain today.

Preparations

Erect the altar in the East and cover it with a light green cloth edged with white, flowery lace. Adorn the ritual place with spring flowers, including Easter lilies or daffodils. Position several empty candleholders on the altar and one unlighted silver taper anointed with Neroli oil in the middle. Place on the pentacle or in a porcelain dish a hard-boiled egg cut into as many segments as celebrants. Next to it, set a goblet of mead or milk punch. Locate the cauldron in the center of the ritual space and fill it with the needfire mix plus gorse. Prepare Morwyn incense, petitions written in red ink on parchment paper, and green tapers consecrated with Pan oil. In addition, coveners bring clay pots with soil and planted with seeds, which they place at the foot of the altar before the rite begins.

Opening the Temple

The Priestess and Priest enter the ritual space alone. The Priestess silently conse-crates the egg and mead as she would do with cakes and ale, and the Priest consecrates the salt and water. Both concentrate on the significance of birth and fertility. The Priestess opens the Circle using the Greater Banishing Pentagram Ritual or the Wicca Way. She signals to the Priest to call the coveners into the room.

They file in one by one with petitions and unlighted tapers in hand (the pots are already by the altar), and circumnambulate the Circle three times, placing their tapers on the altar. As they take their places, the Officers of the Quarters (coveners designated to take charge of each Quarter of the Circle) place the elemental symbols in their appointed positions next to the Quarter candles.

Once settled, all meditate on the meaning of birth, the symbol of the egg, the Green Goddess, the Lord of the Greenwood, and the return of life and hope to the earth and all living things. Appropriate music plays in the background.

The Rite

After a time, the Priestess rings the bell to rouse the others from their reverie.

Priestess: "The Great Wheel of Life has turned, and it is now spring, the time for rebirth and regeneration. The goddess and god await us beneath the greenwood tree; the creatures of the forest emerge from their winter's slumber; the earth puts forth new shoots and foliage. It is time to awaken. Arise, and be reborn!"

The Priestess lights the silver candle, and the coveners go one by one to the altar, light their tapers from the silver one, and place them in holders. As they do so, each member says something spontaneous, such as "Conception time is nigh!"; "Awake from slumber!"; "I am reborn!"; "Life has been renewed!"; or, "It is spring, and the meadows are in flower!"

INVOCATION OF THE QUARTERS

The Officer of the East lights the incense, lifts the censer toward the East, and announces, "On a gentle wind is born the spring season. East is the direction of the rising Sun, which brings sustenance to all life. Great Guardians of the

Eastern Realms of the Universe! I call upon you to guard this sacred gathering. Keep us safe from negativity!"

The Officer of the East walks deosil around the Circle, swinging the censer, and replaces it in the East.

The Officer of the South lights the candle, raises it aloft toward the South, and says, "This flame burning clear and true symbolizes our aspirations and willingness to do! It burns with deep and fiery passion, as the element of fire spurs us into action. Great Guardians of the Southern Realms of the Universe! I call upon you to guard this sacred gathering. Keep us safe from negativity!"

The Officer of the South walks deosil around the Circle with the lighted taper, and places it again in the South.

The Officer of the West raises the chalice of water toward the West and calls, "The gently flowing stream, whose drops form the shining tear of the Sun, nourishes and reanimates all life. It flows within us and bears us onward on our journey. Great Guardians of the Western Realms of the Universe! I call upon you to guard this sacred gathering! Keep us safe from negativity!"

The Officer of the West walks deosil around the Circle, sprinkling water, and replaces the chalice in the West.

The Officer of the North raises the celler of consecrated salt to the North and speaks, "This crystallization of the essence of Mother Earth links us to the land, which is our origin. From the womb of the Great Mother we are born, and to her we return when the purpose of our lives has been accomplished. Let us never forget that to her we owe our existence. Great Guardians of the Northern Realms of the Universe! I call upon you to guard this sacred gathering! Keep us safe from negativity!"

The Officer of the North walks deosil around the Circle, sprinkling salt, and replaces the celler in the North.

INVOCATION OF THE GODDESS

The Priestess goes to the altar and invokes the goddess.

Priestess: "Springtime Maiden, you who are known as Brigit of the Shining Light, Morwyn the Fair, Eostre, and Astarte, bride of the laughing greenwood god, we invoke you to grace us with your presence! Be with us now in all your fresh and pristine beauty, both as a reminder of the springtime of our lives, and as a symbol of the possibilities that await each and every one of us in this exciting New Year!"

INVOCATION OF THE GOD
The Priestess retires and the Priest comes forward, faces the altar, and invokes the god.

Priest: "Lord of the Greenwood, known to some as Robin the Merry, we hear your cloven hooves frolic in the wind and sense your laughter as it echoes through the trees. You are the gladsome springtime god whose buoyant virility attracts the virgin queen. From the sacred union with the goddess is born the Child of Promise, whose glorious life is revealed to us at this season, through the flowering forth of the field, wood, and meadow. Symbol of fertility and life incarnate, be with us now, and infect us with your merriment!"

JUMPING THE CAULDRON
The Priestess comes forward.

Priestess: "We convene today to welcome in the springtime and the flowering of the field, wood, and meadow. Today is the true New Year, as we can tell by the signs of nature—greening grass, the bulbs sending forth their shoots, buds swelling on the trees, and songs of birds. It is an occasion for great happiness, as we shed our winter shrouds and emerge like newborns to walk naked in the into the light of the Sun."

She lights the needfire and continues.

"Let anyone who wishes come forward and make a request by way of petition to the Lord and Lady of the Universe."

Beginning with the Priestess, followed by the Priest, and then the other coveners, who are moving deosil around the Circle, each covener comes forward and throws a petition into the needfire, then jumps the cauldron, shouting, "*Harahaya!*" If they prefer, the Priestess and Priest can lead the coven in a dance around the cauldron when, from time to time, a member casts a petition into the fire, then leaps the cauldron. The signal for the dance to stop comes when each person has jumped the cauldron.

RITE OF PLANTING

After this, the Priest kneels by the pots of earth planted with seeds, raises his hands over the pots, and affirms, "Humble symbols of our as yet unspoken aspirations, you who sleep in the rich loam of Mother Earth, be cleansed of negativity!"

The Priestess cups her hands over the soil and says: "Gestating hopes, ideas, and plans, may you flower forth from the womb of the Great Mother and fulfill the desires of these faithful worshippers."

The Officer of the East censes the pots.

East: "May the gentle breezes refresh your spirit."

The Officer of the South passes the candle over the pots.

South: "May you be imbued with the fire of life."

The Officer of the West waters the pots.

West: "May you be fertile and fruitful."

The Officer of the North sprinkles needfire ashes on the pots, or if these have not yet cooled enough to touch, holds the salt celler over them.

North: "May you ever prosper."

The coveners collect their pots to take home later.

SHARING THE EGG AND MEAD

Priestess: "As symbols of the fertility and creativity, which is part of all nature and so also lives in every one of us, let us eat together the sacred egg and drink the honey mead."

First, she puts aside some egg and sprinkles it with honey mead as a libation to the god and goddess. Then she eats one segment of the egg and sips the mead, passing both egg and mead to the Priest, who partakes and passes them deosil to the next person.

After the ceremony is completed, dancing, healing, scrying, singing or chanting may take place, or the coven may discuss business.

Closing the Temple

When it is time to close, the Priestess performs a banishing ritual. Then she goes to the eastern Quarter.

Priestess, standing with feet apart, athame in right hand, arms raised: "Great Guardians of the Eastern realms of the Universe! We thank you for lending your power and protection to our rite. As you depart to your celestial abodes, we bid you farewell, in perfect love and perfect peace!"

She repeats the process at each Quarter, returns to the East and calls:

"*I. A. O.*" (pronounced 'ee-aahh-ooh'). The rite is ended. Blessed Be!"

Feast and be merry! Each covener returns home with the planted seeds and sees that they prosper. Extinguish the candles and give them to the coveners to take home and relight until they burn down. In this way each one's heart's desire will be fulfilled.

Beltane/May Eve/Rudemas/
Rood Day/St. Walburga's Day
(April 30)

Beltane, the first summer Sabbat, commemorates the planting season and the full flowering of nature. If possible, perform this rite outdoors.

On this date in ancient times, the Celts would gather on a hill overlooking the sea or a lake, and roll a blazing wheel down the slope into the water to dramatize the union of the god and goddess. This is a fertility festival, attested to by the ceremony of the Maypole that celebrates the fertilizing power of the god. During this season, as part of a desire to link with nature, Witches erect woodland shrines and make offerings to the elementals to honor the puissance and majesty of the forest.

They cut the Maypole from ash (symbolic of the life force) and festoon it with flowers, ribbons, herbs, and feathers. Then they all dance around it, invoking the fertilizing powers of the god. This is a merry festival, celebrated with much singing, dancing, games, eating, and drinking. Robert Graves in *The White Goddess* evokes the scene from days of old as follows: "It was the time of beribboned Maypoles, of Collyridian cakes and ales, of wreaths, posies, of lovers' gifts, of archery contests, of meritotters [see-saws] and merribowls [great vats of milk punch]...[and] marriages under the greenwood tree." [22]

Preparations

Erect the altar in the Southeast and cover it with a light green cloth fringed with white lace. Anoint white altar candles with GreenGoddess oil. Place green candles dressed with Pan oil at the Quarters . Also at the Quarters, leave small piles of ash leaves for the Officers of the Quarters to cast to the four directions. Have ready on the altar a bowl of spring flower petals and vervain with which to ring the Circle, and an offering of whole wild ginger root for the elemental spirits.

Burn incense made from angelica, willow bark, lavender, chamomile, geranium flowers, frankincense, myrrh, and benzoin. Also prepare needfire mix and bring a cauldron in which to burn it. Prepare a maibowle for the feast from granulated sugar, white wine, a dash of lemon juice, and a sprig of sweet woodruff. Or concoct a milk punch from the recipe given at the end of this ritual.

The celebrants convene and decorate the Maypole before the rite commences. They bring ribbons, herbs, bows, flowers, etc., to festoon the pole. Play lively dance music like Scottish reels or the more exhilaratingly, fairy-like music of *Anitra's Dance* by Grieg.

When the pole is ready, the Priestess and Priest gather the coveners around the Circle.

Priestess: "Come, merry band, let us rejoice together! Today the goddess resumes her rule over the fertile earth and stimulates us to arise and begin anew a cycle of vitality and productivity."

Meditation

Priest: "Let us pause for a few minutes and imagine we are sitting deep within a primeval forest. It is Spring, and a light breeze is playing through the leaves, evoking the muffled murmurings of the fairies and elementals who surround us. Sweet herbal scents arise from dewy ground, and we are linked with the energy that surges through all living, growing things. We can feel it, smell it, hear it, see it grow. . . ."

Opening of the Temple

After a few minutes, the Priestess rises and opens the Circle in the usual manner.

A pre-selected covener or guest presents the ginger to the elementals and circumscribes the Circle with flower petals and vervain. The presenter should devise a personal offering prayer along the following lines,

Covener: "Spirits of the Four Elements, Air, Fire, Water, and Earth! We welcome you as you caress our cheeks with a shy breeze, warm our bodies with the gentle sun's rays, moisten our skin with the rising dew, and sift the ever shifting sands of time over our feet. To show our gratitude for the services you perform for us, we offer you wild ginger root, ambrosia of your gods. May you continue to serve us well, and may we coexist in peace and harmony. So mote it be!"

Invocation of the Quarters

The Officers of the Quarters invoke the protection of the Archangels of the Quarters in the usual manner. After each Quarter is invoked the Officer gathers some ash leaves, and casts them in the direction of the element.

The Rite

Priestess: "Companions, we are gathered together to celebrate the sacred eve of Beltane, and the flowering forth of the woods and meadows."

INVOCATION OF THE GODDESS

The Priestess faces the altar: "Ineffable goddess, you are the green ground from which all life on this planet emerges. Your emerald depths enfold the mysteries of creation. Today you welcome the fertile passion of the god-fire. Today we hail this brilliant union. Come unto us in your full flowering, maiden made woman, give us your star-bright blessing!"

East: "Open our minds with the winds of knowledge."
South: "May our wills merge with the Divine Will."

West: "Ever shall we seek to understand the mysteries of the Universe."

North: "And dwell as one with the trees, skies, and waters of this Earth."

All: "Be with us here and now!"

INVOCATION OF THE GOD

As the Priestess retires the Priest comes forward and lights the needfire.

Priest: "Sun-strong Apollo, you who inflame the goddess with your passion and luminescence; creator, diviner, healer; we invoke you to ignite us with your fire-tongue rays, and emblazon us with your might. Through the forces of nature we taste your glory and our spirits sway with dancing."

RITE OF THE MAYPOLE

All stand and link hands. Moving clockwise around the Maypole, coveners chant *"harahaya"* and dance—first slowly, then quicker and quicker. Soon the Priest drops out of the Circle and recites above the voices.

Priest: "As it was in days of old
　　　　We dance around the May Day pole
　　　　Waking sleepers to the light
　　　　Our heart beats skip into the night
　　　　Field and forest, stream and tree
　　　　May Earth's delights forever be
　　　　Impressed upon our hearts and minds
　　　　As our souls swirl throughout all time."

The Priest repeats this chant several times. At the proper moment everyone lets go of each other's hands and directs energy toward the Maypole, then all fall to the ground.

Priestess, after a moment: "Gaze upon the Maypole now and see in your mind's eye the gleaming life force reach up through the earth and cascade overhead. Feel it shimmer through us and flow from us into the greenwood. Thus, we are at one with the god-fire."

All remain transfixed by the image for several minutes. After a time, the Priestess sounds a bell. Everyone is invited to share a vision aloud.

Closing the Temple
The Priestess closes the Temple in the usual manner and banishes spirits to their dominions. Feast and be merry!

Here are two traditional recipes for the Beltane feast.

Picau Ar y Maen (Welsh Cakes)
1 lb. flour
3/4 c. sugar
1/2 t. allspice
1/4 t. cinnamon
1 t. baking powder
1/8 t. salt
1 c. butter
1 egg, slightly beaten
2 T. milk
1/2 cup mixed dried fruit

Combine the dry ingredients; set aside. Cream the butter, and add the egg and milk. Slowly add the dry ingredients. Mix in the fruit. This will make a sticky dough. Roll out the dough on a floured board to a thickness of 1/4 inch, and cut into rounds. Cook on a greased griddle for about 3 minutes on each side until golden brown. Cool and sprinkle with castor sugar. Serve alone or with butter. [23]

Milk Punch
1 cup half-and-half
1 egg

dash salt

1 t. sugar

dash vanilla

1 shot whisky

Beat the ingredients together, pour into a bowl, and sprinkle with nutmeg.

Summer Solstice or Alban Hefin
(June 19-22)

The longest day of the year ushers in the Summer Solstice, when the Sun is at its zenith for the year. Mysterious shadows rustle through the trees, and the compelling Pan pipes echo deep within the forest. Elves, fairies, and other woodland creatures meet to rejoice on Midsummer Night's Eve. The Sun god is at his most potent now. However, as soon as the Sun reaches its apex, it begins its long decline, and eventually ebbs away into nothingness to be reborn again at the Winter Solstice. Both the living and the dying gods are honored on this day. The living deity is called the Oak King, the Dying God, the Holly King.

On this day, collect herbs, especially St. John's Wort, as the concentration of oils in the leaves is at its strongest now. It is said that if a Witch jumps naked over a blooming St. John's Wort herb on Summer Solstice Eve, she will be pregnant within a year. In Brazil, at this time of year (St. John's Night) young people gather in homes and read each other's fortunes, then go outdoors to launch balloons in which lighted candles have been placed to illuminate the nighttime sky.

Coveners entwine garlands of summer flowers to wear as crowns, and prepare pumpernickel bread to eat at the rite as a symbol of the brown, fertile earth. Bring white heather to mark the Quarters, and an herb to cast into the needfire. The herb each participant chooses should embody some characteristic that its offerer finds significant. For example, chamomile is associated with the strength of the Sun, and might be chosen by one who wishes to heal others with solar power, or conversely, desires to draw solar energy.

Preparations

Erect the altar in the South; cover it with a diaphanous, silvery, or pastel cloth. Place white heather at the Quarters, and wild mountain thyme in a silver bowl on the altar. Anoint silver altar candles with Tree Elf oil, and burn wisteria and pine incense. Celtic harp music sets the mood. Coveners wear pastel-colored robes and wreaths of flowers. When all have taken their appointed places in the Circle, the Priestess begins.

Priestess: "A pretty eve this is for elves, fairies, and blithe spirits. Their laughter sparkles on forest leaves, and their merriment touches our beings, eliciting our most secret thoughts and desires. Magic is borne on the summer breeze, and anything is possible tonight. So, I bid you welcome to this Circle of Light. May we, if but only briefly, become as one with the gods of old. Here, now, tonight!"

Opening the Temple

The Priestess opens the Circle using the Wicca Way.

Another covener offers fresh thyme to the elemental spirits, first by ringing the Circle with the herb (begin and end in the East), and then places some of the herb on the altar.

Covener: "Elemental spirits of wind, fire, water, and earth! You who are called dryads, nyads, salamanders, gnomes, sylphs, and elves. I bring you this token of wild mountain thyme, bounty of the Earth Mother. May your energies pulse in harmony with cosmic life, and may you be at peace with humanity. I also lay this offering so that you will lend your powers to the success of this rite."

Invocation of the Goddess

Priestess: "Supernal Queen of Heaven and Mother of us all, from whose dark and fertile womb we are born, and to whom we will return, shine your radiant smile upon this Circle, and grace us with your appearance! Your mysteries are ineffable, as ancient as life itself. You hold within your breast the key to the secret of life. Show us the way to wisdom, and help us live proper Wicca lives!"

Invocation of the God
Priest: "Eternal Lord of the Universe, you whose existence reminds us that in our endings we find new beginnings, we invoke you to be with us at this rite! At this season, your strength is at its apex. But within this concentration of power lies the seed of your own destruction. Henceforth, your potency begins to ebb until it folds in upon itself and disappears. As the Wheel of Life ever turns, so you will be reborn as the Child of Promise, symbol of everlasting life. Oak King of the Waxing Year, Holly King of the Waning Year, we welcome you both into this Circle, and we accept your energies into our lives!"

Rite of the Sacred Herbs
Priestess: "One of the great secrets that the goddess revealed to humanity, and particularly to Witches, is the occult knowledge of wortcunning. We are ever grateful to her for showing us how to use herbs in Magic and healing. As this is the season when herbal essences are at their most highly concentrated levels, we commemorate the occasion. It is time to bring forth the herbs we have brought to this Circle, briefly describe their significances, and cast the plants into the needfire. As we perform this ceremony, we will each make a secret wish associated with the realm of fertility—keyword of the season—and we shall will that the fragrant incense smoke created by the burning herbs carries our petitions to the gods where they will find favor."

The Priestess lights the needfire, takes her herb, describes its powers, makes a silent wish, and drops the plant into the fire. Every covener concentrates intently at the moment when the herbs are being consumed to help propel the wishes on their way. Any herbs will suffice for this ritual, but most appropriate choices include: thyme, rue, chamomile, St. John's Wort, fern, vervain, elderberry, mistletoe, motherwort, calendula, mugwort, and white heather. Generally the wishes are for physical fertility, enhanced mental acumen, increased creativity, inspiration, development of psychic powers—anything that deals with fertility of body, mind, or spirit.

Closing the Temple

The Priestess bids the Guardians of the Quarters farewell and closes the Circle. The celebrants feast, make merry, practice scrying, search for magical herbs in the forest, dance, play music, etc.

Lammas or Lughnassad
(August 1)

Occurring on August 1, Lammas is considered the first harvest festival; for it is at this time in northern climes that farmers begin to reap grain. Our coven views this rite as the precursor of the harvest season, which ends with Hallowmas. The union of the god and goddess on this day ensures fertility of mind and body as well as a fruitful harvest in the season to come. In ancient times, Celts would climb a hill to perform the ritual and symbolically—or even actually—sacrifice a male representation of the god in a burning wicker basket to encourage bountiful crops. Certainly it is still the season for rites of material increase, and the nature charms we devise should be for that purpose.

By tradition at Lammastide, the country folk gathered at harvest fairs to sell food and livestock, and to participate in games of strength and prowess, dancing, and feasting.

If you live near a body of water—be it a well, stream, lake, or ocean—you might wish to revive an ancient custom and journey to the water, partake of its inherent healing qualities (especially at sacred wells), and thank the spirits of the site by leaving behind garlands of acacia, asters, and holly.

Preparations

Prepare the needfire from oak, ash, holly, hawthorn, cherry, rowan, fir, pine, and birch. This is also a good season to forage for materials to replenish your needfire mix. Make an incense from green base, aloes wood, myrtle leaves, musk oil, and a dash of elderberry wine (also a fine incense for love petitions). Play light but compelling music, such as Self-Realization Fellowship's *Divine Gypsy* as background music.

Circumscribe the Circle with scarlet oak leaves (the Druidic tree of the month), and place a cyclamen plant on the altar (symbolic of a long and fruitful marriage of the Lord and Lady). Set the altar in the Southwest, and cover it with a harvest green altar cloth edged with gold braid. Embroider or paint it with representations of corn, wheat, or barley. Altar candles usually are yellow (astral color of the season), green (fertility, fruition), or red (passion, health). Anoint them with amber oil (Venus).

Celebrants dress in robes of any color except black, and bring the following foods, or any dish concocted from seasonal fruits, vegetables and grains: corn bread, barley cakes, grilled carrots, stewed tomatoes, bean casserole, apricot pie, peach cobbler. The cakes and ale consumed during the ceremony symbolize the mystery of the grain transformed into life-sustaining bread and brew.

The nature charms relate to creativity, fertility, love, and union. They draw and synthesize these energies. Coveners bring the following items to make the nature charms: seven grains of barley, a beth root, a pinch of dittany of Crete, patchouli oil.

Meditation

After gathering around the altar in a Circle, the coven sits and meditates on harvest, fruition, and the union of the god and goddess.

Opening of the Temple

The Priestess opens the Temple in the Wicca Way and invokes the Guardians of the Quarters.

INVOCATION OF THE GODDESS

Priestess: "Celestial and most lovely Lady, goddess of love and fertility! We invoke you in this sacred hour to be present with us in our worship. Today we celebrate the moment of your fruitful marriage with the god. Bathed in golden light, displaying silver rings, the goddess slips through secret glades toward this holy union. From the consummation among dewy, dark green ferns and silent oaks, beneath the radiant heavens is conceived the Child of Promise. From this day forth the Child quickens within the serene womb of the Great Mother to be born unto humankind. Blessed Lady, this is your moment! You hold the power of manifestation within your body. Today you are most beautiful in the achievement of your precious miracle. We invoke you in the power and the glory of the one eternal Life of which we are all a part!"

INVOCATION OF THE GOD

Priest: "Fertile and abundant Lord of the Universe! From your seed we are born. You are the essence creation. Tonight you direct your energy to the consummation of the holy union with your bride. And we rejoice; for from this joining is brought forth the Child of Promise to nurture all life. May your creative force permeate us all as drops of dew condensing on the mossy forest carpet. May we become worthy vessels for this joyous gift."

PRAYER

Priestess: "We gather for the festival of Aphrodite to celebrate the marriage of the god and goddess and the conception of the Child of Light. As we rejoice on this felicitous occasion, let us heed that we have served the Lord and Lady well; for as the Wheel of Life's seasons come round, we will find that we have reaped as we have sown. May the fruits of our toil within the Wheel's full turn reflect the love labor we have earnestly performed in our quest of the Celestial Path. May we work to merit the harvest bestowed upon us by the goddess, and may our hearts and minds then be prepared to receive the Child of Promise openly and without fear in perfect love and perfect trust."

Rite of the Cakes and Ale

The Priestess consecrates the cakes and ale.

Priestess: "Let us partake of the traditional cakes and ale, symbols of the mystery of the transformation of grain into sustenance."

She holds her Athame over the plate of cakes and exorcises it.

Priestess: "Substance of the earth, I cleanse you of negativity."

The Priestess repeats the procedure over the goblet of ale. Returning to the cakes, she touches them with the athame and says:

"Product of the earth, I consecrate you. May you serve to nourish and sustain life."

She repeats this gesture and words with the ale. Then she crumbles some cake on the ground to the left, right, and center of the altar, and sprinkles some ale in a similar manner, and proclaims:

"Lord and Lady of earth, sea, and sky! We offer you this libation. Partake of it in good health, as it is freely given as a token of our esteem. May your union be full of delight, and may you always look with favor upon this Circle of initiates!"

Rite of the Nature Charms

The Priestess lights the needfire. The coveners bring out ingredients for nature charms. The Priest passes around the Circle a vial of patchouli oil for each person to anoint the beth root; coveners then enclose it in a mojo bag with the other herbs. The Priest gathers the bags, sprinkles them with salt and water, and then passes them through the needfire smoke pronouncing over each one: "I hereby consecrate you with the salt of the earth, water of the heavens, searing flame, and fragrant smoke. May you help bring about ——'s (covener's name) most cherished dream."

He returns the bags to the owners so that they may carry them in a pocket or purse.

Closing the Temple

The Priestess closes the Temple in the usual manner, and banishes spirits and unseen guests to their abodes. The rite is over. Feast and be merry! By tradition, celebrants participate in lively dancing to celebrate the marriage of the god and goddess. Wicca couples often slip off into the forest now and perform the Great Rite (love-making).

Autumn Equinox or Alban Elfed
(September 19—22)

As the Sun enters Libra, sign of cosmic justice and balance, the days grow shorter, the nights lengthen, and the Earth finds itself relentlessly drawn toward autumn and dusk. On the Autumn Equinox Witches offer thanks for the material and spiritual harvest they reaped throughout the year. It is an introspective season, during which we assess our progress on the Path of Light and rededicate ourselves to the Wicca Way. Consequently, Alban Elfed is the best time of all for initiation.

Take advantage of the equinoctal tides to achieve inner balance. To this end our coven often performs together the Middle Pillar Ritual.[24] We also prepare dollies from sheaths of corn which we consecrate and keep until spring, when we take them to the field and plow them into the earth to insure fertile crops.

Preparations

The ruler of the dying season is Saturn, and the god and goddess forms include Arwan, Cernunnos, Centaur, Cheiron, Demeter, and Persephone.

Decorate the altar with symbols of these deities and signs of the harvest such as sheaths of wheat, dried fruit, pine cones, acorns, dried corn husks, squash, and other gourds. Drape the altar with a Libra-green cloth edged with gold. Flank the altar with green candles anointed with white rose and violet oil. To the right of the altar, place a small pile of colorful leaves and a broom as a symbol of the knowledge and wisdom gained throughout the year. An appropriate incense for the occasion is pine and patchouli with a hint of rose and strawberry oils.

To make the corn dollies, everyone should bring a corn husk, strong thread, and colorful ribbon and lace to shape the head, arms, and legs; dried flowers to decorate the head in a garland; and if desired, calico cloth to wrap around the body as a skirt or dress. Also have on hand parchment paper on which to write your petition for the needfire during the rededication rite.

Besides performing initiations at this Sabbat, our coven transfers the scepter of authority on the Autumn Equinox. Since we believe that each covener benefits and learns from the experience of directing the coven for one year, we share this privilege and responsibility. The symbol of the Priest or Priestess is a simple scepter or staff that resembles a walking stick into which we carve various names of power and symbols. This aspect of the Equinox ritual is optional.

Meditation

The Priestess lights the altar candles. The group sits in the Circle to meditate on the fruits of their personal, physical, psychic, and spiritual labors. They also consider the meaning of autumn and its reflection in all people who experience, learn, mature, and apply their acquired intelligence during the autumn of their lives. Vivaldi's *Four Seasons* provides inspirational background music.

Opening the Temple

After a while the Priestess rises and opens the Temple. She goes to the Northeast Quadrant, raises the pointed index finger of her left hand above her head, and points her athame to the earth, thereby grounding the power. She declares:

"As it was in the Time
Of the beginning
So it is now!
Goddess of the field
And God of the hunt
All power of the element is yours [25]
I hereby declare open

This Alban Elfed Circle!"

INVOCATION OF THE GODDESS

Priestess: "Goddess of the blond field, borne on the harvest wind, I enjoin you to descend upon this gathering and whisper to us your secret counsel which you have concealed in the rows of heavy-headed grain. Assist us to balance both our inner selves and the outer world so that life as you have conceived it can continue to flourish. By the power of your love may we be able to convince others that all our lives and the essence of life, itself depend on ecological balance."

INVOCATION OF THE GOD

Priest: "Agile stalker of field, forest, mountain, and stream, you whose quick arrow can instantly paralyze and destroy life, I petition you to attend this gathering and reveal to us the true meaning of your awesome might. Teach us to realize the consequences of our esoteric and exoteric acts, and to bear responsibility for our actions."

RITE OF THE TRANSFERENCE OF THE SCEPTER

The initiates stand, and the Priestess goes to the Northeast with the scepter of authority.

Priestess: "The Wheel of the Year inexorably turns, and in this way, time passes. Once again, we must select from among us a new leader to direct the great work of this coven. (Here the Priestess may add personal observations such as what follows.) This year during which I have cherished the scepter has been full of wondrous experiences. I have learned what it means to be imbued with the exhilaration of power, and also realize the enormous responsibility that accompanies authority. As with all things, my term as director of this group is at an end, and gladly I choose a successor. I hereby name——(new Priestess) to replace me, and relinquish to her the scepter of power."

The new leader steps forward, the former Priestess hands over the staff, and the two exchange places with the successor now standing in the Northeast. At this time, the new leader may make a speech of thanks, receive hugs and congratulations from coveners, or whatever seems appropriate.

When the well-wishing has died down, the Officers of the Quarters resume their places and raise aloft the symbols of their elements. The new Priestess continues the Equinox rite according to a ritual taken from Israel Regardie's *The Golden Dawn.*

OBSERVANCE OF THE EQUINOX
Priestess: "Let us consecrate according to the ancient custom the return of the Equinox."

East, raising the censer: "Light."

West, raising the chalice: "Darkness."

East: "East."

West: "West."

East: "Air."

West: "Water."

The Priestess knocks with the scepter in middle of Circle: "I am the Reconciler between them."

South, raising the salt: "Heat."

North, raising the celler: "Cold."

South: "South."

North: "North."

South: "Fire."

North: "Earth."

Priestess, knocking with the scepter: "I am the Reconciler between them."

East: "One Creator."

South: One Preserver."

West: "One Destroyer."

North: "One Redeemer."

Priestess, knocking with the scepter: One Reconciler between them."[26]

MIDDLE PILLAR RITUAL

The coveners sit, and the Priestess begins.

Priestess: "Imagine yourselves sitting in a great Temple of ancient times facing West. The Black Pillar of Binah—severity, the unseen—is on your right, and the White Pillar of Chokmah—mercy, manifestation—is on your left. You strike the perfect balance between them, and through chanting and visualization, you create the Middle Pillar of beneficence."

The coveners intone together the Middle Pillar Ritual, repeating each god name several times. All the while, they visualize the appropriately colored lights at their chakras and the rush of energy down the middle of their bodies from head to toe. When this segment of the ritual is complete, all remain still for a while, contemplating the perfect balance of energy.

RITE OF REDEDICATION

The Priestess rises and lights the needfire.

Priestess: "Each of us has chosen the balanced path of Wicca to guide us on our journey. Today we rededicate ourselves and our souls to the Wicca Way. To this end I ask you each to step forward, reaffirm your intentions, and petition the Lord and Lady to help you achieve a single goal within one full turn of the Wheel."

The Priestess begins by stepping forward: "I swear by this sacred fire that I,——(name), Priestess and Witch, shall ever be true to the principles embodied by the god and goddess, and that I shall endeavor always to walk in the light of the lantern of Wicca."

The others follow suit, add their offerings to the fire, and declare in their own words their rededication to the path.

RITE OF THE CORN DOLLIES

When the petitions have been cast into the fire, the Priestess brings out the materials to make the corn dollies. After completing the dollies, each covener, beginning with the Priestess, passes a dolly through incense smoke, over a candle flame, and sprinkles it with consecrated water, salt, and elderberry wine, saying:

"I hereby purify and consecrate you with this fragrant smoke of the gods. May the desire infused in you rise to the heavens.

"I hereby purify and consecrate you with the cleansing flame. May your purpose burn ever bright throughout the eons until it is fulfilled.

"I hereby purify and consecrate you with the goddess-given element of water. As water sustains life, so may you nourish the wish implanted in you.

"I hereby purify and consecrate you with the salt of the earth. May the purpose with which you are endowed take root on the plane of manifestation.

"I baptize you with this sacred wine to activate you, and hereby name you——(name of corn dolly). May you fulfill the purpose for which you were created."

Hold the dolly in both hands, blow on it three times, and say:

"Be instilled with the breath of life. May you spark my endeavors."

Place the corn dolly in a shoebox-like container, and keep it hidden away until spring when you may plow it into a cultivated field or your garden. If you do not have a garden, keep the dolly by your bed or desk to inspire you throughout the winter, and consign it to the needfire on the Spring Equinox.

Closing the Temple

The new High Priestess closes the Temple in the traditional Wicca Way. The rite is ended. Feast and be merry!

Hallowmas or Samhain
(October 31)

Hallowmas, or Samhain (pronounced "sow-en") is the best known and probably least understood Sabbat. In the popular imagination, Witches swathe themselves in black and journey on broomsticks to secret gatherings held on windswept mountain tops or in inky forests where they indulge in frenzied Saturnalias to invoke Satan and his minions. Such debauched behavior could not be farther from the truth. Hallowmas is the most solemn Sabbat occasion, when Witches mourn and honor their deceased ancestors and pray for inner guidance throughout the dark winter that lies ahead. Witches dress in black because absence of color represents both death and a deep meditational state. At Hallowmas, we observe that in our endings we find new beginnings, and reaffirm the continuance of life. This concept is reflected in the black altar cloth, symbol of death, edged with red, to represent life. Other translations of the name for this festival include "Fire of Peace," "Summer's End," and "Assembly of Spirits," all of which capture the "spirit," so to speak, of the event.

Hallowmas is the only Sabbat that we must perform precisely on the date, because Witches believe that only then a window is open between this plane and those planes inhabited by spirits, and it is possible to travel astrally to the worlds beyond, or to allow spirits to visit the material plane to bring us messages. Formerly, Pagans left part of their suppers by the fire to nourish dead kin and other wandering spirits who might be attracted to the hearth fire on that night.

Take an apple to be blessed by the Priestess and Priest during the ceremony. Once you return home, put a mirror on your altar with two lighted black candles on either side. If possible, place a third candle behind you. At the stroke of midnight, eat the apple while looking into the mirror. By the time you finish the apple, a vision of your Higher Self may appear to you in the mirror.

Preparations

Place the altar in the Northwest and cover it with a black cloth bordered with red. Flank the altar with two black candles anointed with patchouli and myrrh oil. Decorate the altar with corn sheaves, dried flowers and reeds, pumpkins, and hazelnuts (the fruit of the tree of wisdom, from whose branches we cut the wand of transformation). Our coven uses a black mirror for scrying during the ceremony. For directions on how to prepare a black mirror see *Secrets of a Witch's Coven*.

The Samhnagen needfire is composed of the usual nine sacred woods plus fern, gorse, and straw. A white beacon candle anointed with rose oil stands just outside the Circle (Northwest) to draw the spirits. Burn Witches' Circle incense or prepare your own from myrrh pieces, patchouli, pine, and wormwood to which you may add cedarwood, rose, and myrrh oils. Ring the Circle with Solomon's seal herb as an offering to the elementals. Gregorian chants make suitable background music.

Coveners bring an apple, candleholder, and a black taper anointed with cedarwood oil. Only black robes are permitted at this rite! For the feast prepare traditional harvest dishes of roast pork, mulled, spiced wine (with which to drink toasts for the coming year), and hazelnut cake.

Meditation

It is the custom among Witches at Hallowmas to go to a lonely shore at the edge of the forest, or to a vast meadow where the horizons and the land merge into one indistinguishable mass. Weather permitting, our coven seeks such a place for a half-hour's meditation before we return indoors for the ceremony. Since the keyword for this Sabbat is "completion," appropriate subjects for meditation include what the harvest has reaped, in what direction the personal and universal soul of the coven is headed, and reincarnation. Before leaving for the meditation we fortify ourselves with mugs of steamy Psychic Vision tea, which is mugwort tea to which we add some eyebright, bay laurel leaves, powdered ginseng root, a pinch of wormwood, and honey.

Opening the Temple

The Priestess opens the Circle using the Greater Pentagram Ritual. You must use this powerful ritual at this particular Sabbat. Officers of the Quarters purify the Circle with their symbolic elements, and invoke the Guardians of the Quarters.

The Priestess stands in the northwest Quarter before the altar, and proclaims:

"This is a time that is not a time
In a place that is not a place,

On a day that is not a day,
Between the worlds
And beyond." [27]

The Priestess anoints the third eye of each covener with Occult Contact oil and carries the beacon candle around the Circle three times. The initiates follow while she speaks.

Priestess: "With this web of light I strengthen the bond between you and your ancestors this Samhain night."

The Priestess lights the needfire in the center of the Circle. Beginning with the Priestess, all light black tapers from the needfire, then stand in a circle around the needfire, and repeat,

All: "We are the bridge between the worlds and need only extend our hands in welcome to draw the spirits forth. By the power of the elements, we demand the spirits manifest and share this Samhain night with us!"

The coveners slowly walk the Circle three times, while the Priestess invokes the goddess at the altar. If the initiates finish before the Priestess and Priest are through with their invocations, they sit in their places and contemplate the altar or the needfire, visualizing the flame enveloping their bodies and minds, and travel to the depths of their souls.

INVOCATION OF HECATE
Priestess: "Hecate, Lady of darkness and mystery, high priestess of the concealed silver star, divine light that rules in darkness! Appear to us tonight and dwell in our hearts that we may share in your power and be true channels of your strength. Bless this rite and grant that the spirits be with us!"

INVOCATION OF THE GOD
Priest: "Lord of the flickering shadows, you who are also the Lord of life, triumphant over death, open the gates through which all must pass and let those who have gone before us return this night to share the Samhain feast!"

RITE FOR THE DEAD
All: "Blessed be our remembered dead who are bound to us by the Circle of Life.

May these and all souls find peace and complete fulfillment in the Divine Light."

The coveners affix their candles in holders on the altar, and return to their places. Anyone who wishes to publicly remember a deceased loved one speaks at this time.

DIVINATION

The Priest removes the needfire and the Priestess brings out the coven's large black mirror for divination. She places it in the center of the Circle.

Priestess: "Let our loved ones now passed over to other planes communicate with us, if they will, through the magic mirror. Dwellers on the planes of Light, speak to us, beam wisdom and healing into this mystical Circle."

All intone: "*I A O.*"

Coveners join hands around the mirror, chanting *EN TO PAN*. At the climax of the chant, everybody directs the accumulated energy toward the mirror, then contemplates its fathomless depths. Finally, the Priestess arouses the coveners by ringing a bell three times. Anyone is free to share a vision with the rest of the group.

BLESSING THE APPLES

The Priestess and Priest take the apples from the altar and form a small circle with them at the foot of the altar. The Priest carves a Celtic cross in each apple; the Priestess cuts a circle around them. Next they kneel over the apples, one on each side, clasping over the apples one right hand to the other's left hand. They hold their athames in their free hands, blades pointed downward toward the apples.

Priest: "By this ancient symbol of the encircled cross, fruit of the tree of knowledge, we exorcise you of negativity. Be purified so that you may nourish both body and spirit with your tender, tangy flesh."

Priestess: "Druidic fruit of immortality, you who hold the powers of divination in your cores, be consecrated. May you serve as vehicles by which to reveal to these Witches communications from their Holy Guardian Angels." (After the rite is ended, take home your apple to perform the spell outlined in the description of this ritual.)

Closing the Temple

The Priestess closes the Circle using the Greater Banishing Ritual, then declares,

"Though we extinguish the flames of this Circle of Light in the mundane world, our Samhain fire still dances on the inner planes. Once again, we draw down the veil between the worlds, but the joy of our journey in the realms beyond remains in our memories to gladden our hearts. The rite is ended. Feast and be merry!"

Sabbat Planner

As you probably have surmised from the foregoing rituals, the symbols and other paraphernalia required for the Sabbat rites are many. In order to help you plan your own rituals and to give you a quick reference guide, I provide this Sabbat Planner.

Winter Solstice

Names: Alban Arthan, Yule
Key Phrase: rebirth
Druidic Month: Ruis
Number: 13
Time of Day: midnight
Location: North
Ruler: Capricorn
Colors: black/white
Celtic Bird: rook
God/dess Forms: Isis, the child Horus
Tree: yew; silver fir; elder
Incenses: Enchanted Forest; frankincense; myrrh; benzoin
Plants: pine; holly; mistletoe
Altar Cloth: silver and gold with holly decorations
Robes: white; red; green
Music: Wagner's *Lohengrin*

Candlemas

Names: Oilmec; Imbolg; Feast of the Waxing Light; Lady Day
Key Phrase: quickening
Druidic Month: Luis

Number: 2
Time of Day: pre-dawn; the graying sky
Location: Northeast
Ruler: Aquarius
Colors: red; orange; gold
Celtic Bird: duck
Goddess Forms: Brigit; Persephone; Venus
Tree: rowan (mountain ash)
Incense: Persephone
Plants: chrysanthemums; yellow daisies; marigolds
Altar Cloth: orange with embroidered fire tattvas
Robes: red, orange
Music: Patrick Ball's *Celtic Harp*

Spring Equinox

Names: Alban Eilir, Festival of the Trees
Keyword: birth
Druidic Month: Fearn
Number: 4
Time of Day: dawn
Location: East
Ruler: Aries
Colors: green, the color of freshly plowed earth
Celtic Bird: gull
God/dess forms: Pan; Bran; Hercules (the child); Kore; Morwyn; Persephone;
   Aphrodite; Arianhod; Eostre; Diana
Tree: alder
Incense: Morwyn, to which dittany of Crete is added
Plants: spring flowers; daffodils; hyacinths; Easter lily; crocus
Altar Cloth: light green with white flowered lace border
Robes: pastels
Music: Grieg's *Morning Song*

Beltane

Name: May Eve, Roodmas
Keyword: polarity
Druidic Month: Saille
Number: 5
Time of Day: mid-morning
Location: Southeast
Ruler: Taurus
Colors: green, bright yellow
Celtic Bird: hawk
God/dess Forms: the young Merlin; Marduk (Babylonian fertility god) Cernunnos; Saturn; Pan; Apollo; Brigit; Walburg (earth mother) Artemis (agriculture); Juno (marriage); Bast (pleasure; benign heat of the Sun)
Trees: willow (osier); oak; hawthorn
Incenses: Gypsies' Gold; Green Goddess; or a mixture of geranium leaves, frankincense, benzoin, myrrh, angelica, lavender, vervain, chamomile
Plants: African ginger; ash leaves; angelica; fennel; thyme; rice
Altar Cloth: same cloth as that used at the Spring Equinox, or a bright yellow cloth with a green border
Robes: pastels or fire colors
Music: Vangelis' *Chariots of Fire*

Summer Solstice

Name: Alban Hefir
Keyword: fertilization
Druidic Month: Duir
Time of Day: noon
Location: South
Ruler: Cancer
Trees: oak, holly
Incenses: Sabbat Fire, or frankincense and chamomile
Plants: heather; mistletoe; midsummer fern; mugwort; St. Johnswort; elder-

berries; roses; chamomile; geranium; vervain; elecampane; fennel; thyme; rue

Altar Cloth: a diaphanous cloth of a light material to resemble fairy wings

Robes: bright colors or pastels

Music: Mendelssohn's *Midsummer Night's Dream*

Lammas

Name: Lughnassadh, Festival of the Harvest

Keyword: increase

Druidic Month: Tinne

Number: 8

Time of Day: sunset

Location: Southwest

Ruler: Leo

Colors: yellow, red, green

Celtic Bird: starling

God/dess forms: Binah; Isis; Demeter; Aphrodite; Juno; Hathor; Ishtar; Chokmah; Amon; Saturn; Cernunnos

Trees: scarlet oak, holly

Incenses: Heart's Desire, or a mixture of aloes, myrtle, acacia, and musk

Plants: fruits and vegetables harvested at this time , such as corn, barley, hops, etc.; meadowsweet, beth root, acacia, elderberry, aster, cyclamen, wheat

Altar Cloth: forest green with a gold fringe

Robes: harvest colors; rust; brown; or white

Music: Self-Realization Fellowship's *The Divine Gypsy*

Fall Equinox

Name: Alban Elfed

Keyword: joy

Druidic Month: Muin

Number: 11
Time of Day: dusk
Location: West
Ruler: Libra
Colors: harvest green, rust-red
Celtic Bird: titmouse
God Forms: Arwan; Wrn (Saturn); Cernunnos; Cheirion; Centaur
Trees: aspen; vine; bramble
Incense: Witches' Circle, Middle Pillar
Plants: vine (for the grape harvest), bistort (a Saturnian plant for psychic development)
Altar Cloth: harvest green with gold fringe. You may use the same altar cloth as you used for Lammas
Robes: green, rust
Music: Vivaldi's *Four Seasons*

Hallowmas

Names: Samhain, All Hallows, Festival of the Goddess.
Keyword: completion
Druidic Month: Ngetal (also Peith)
Number: 12
Time of Day: night
Location: Northwest
Ruler: Scorpio
Color: black
Celtic Bird: goose
God/dess forms: Isis; Hecate; Demeter; Holda; Cerridwen; Morrighan; Odin; Bran; Dagda; Osiris
Trees: reed, hazel, water elder
Incenses: Midnight Vision; Ravenwood; Occult Contact; or a mixture of wormwood, cedarwood, myrrh, bay, frankincense, vervain, fir needles, Solomon's seal, benzoin, patchouli, mastic

Plants: Solomon's seal; nutmeg; mint; heliotrope; wormwood; dittany of
   Crete; eyebright; lovage; laurel; bay; pumpkin; ginseng; heliotrope;
   bistort
Altar Cloth: black with red edging
Robes: black
 Music: Gregorian Chants

Chapter Five

Occasional Rituals and Spells

The preceding two chapters dealt with seasonal and lunar rituals practiced regularly in one form or another by most covens. This chapter concerns rites to be practiced for specific purposes. All the rituals have been performed by our coven in response to a need or a request by another covener or someone outside the group. The occasions include rituals to ease the pain of an abortion; create a chalice of light; annihilate a cancerous growth; uncross someone; influence another; attract a mate; recall past lives.

Before you undertake any ritual or spell you need to balance yourself in body and mind. Such "centering" produces the most effective ritual work. To this end I include the following exercises to help you reach a balance with the ebb and flow of the universal tides of the cosmos.

Exercises to Counteract Depression and Negativity

In spite of all our efforts to equilibrate ourselves, even Witches sometimes fall into states of depression induced by tension, anxiety, fatigue, and the general negativity that surrounds us in the modern world. When we find ourselves in such a frame of mind, it becomes difficult to maintain the positive, detached attitude essential for the success of any ritual. The following mini-exercises will help you to combat depression. Although they do not promise to cure what ails you, they will help to dispel surface negative energy and enable you to perform more effectively the rituals and spells that follow in this grimoire.

To discover whether you are at odds with the Universe, sit in a straight-backed chair with your arms at your sides and your feet planted firmly on the ground. Close your eyes, raise your left arm to shoulder level, and hold it there. With your eyes still closed, try to lift your right arm to the same level. Open your eyes. If both arms are at equal height, congratulations! But if they are not, perform the exercises that follow.

Snap-Away Negativity

If, as a child, you were ever called to the principal's office for misbehaving, or if you have had to endure a nerve-wracking interview to further your career, you probably recognize the sinking feeling in the pit of your stomach (often accompanied by perspiration and light-headedness) that materializes as you approach the dreaded door behind which the symbol of authority awaits. The next time you find yourself in such a situation, snap your fingers and clap your hands three times before entering the room. You will be amazed at how the tension dissipates.

Psychic Isometrics

Whenever you feel you are not at one with the universe, perform this simple exercise. Slowly inhale for seven counts, and imagine that a bright white light enters your right foot and travels up the right side of your body to your head as you take in the air. Hold your breath for four counts. Then exhale, counting backwards aloud from seven to one, all the while willing the light to rush down the left side of your body and push out accumulated negativity through your left foot.

Repeat the procedure, this time, counting the exhalation mentally. If you do not find relief, repeat both steps once more.

White Light Defense

If you are extraordinarily depressed or confused, assume a boxer's stance. Clenching both fists tightly, and raising your right fist to the sky, open your right hand and cause a ball of white universal light to enter it. Visualize the white light clearly. Clench your right fist again, and hold on to the positive force. Affirm aloud, "I am positive." Lower both arms to your sides; shake out your hands with fingers open to relieve the tension. You have created a pillar of light and life within yourself.

Never undertake the following or any ritual without first balancing your body and psyche. The above exercises help relieve surface tension. However, they are not a substitute for contemplation and meditation.

Rituals and Spells

Ritual on the Occasion of an Abortion

Our coven believes that it is not for us to mandate when and how a life is taken away from the womb. However, if a woman has made the decision to have an abortion, we perform this ritual to ease her pain and to help send the soul of the fetus back to the womb of the Great Mother, where it will wait to be reborn.

ITEMS REQUIRED

Persephone incense; black altar candles anointed with Hecate oil; a pine cone; two lengths of red yarn (one for the patient's wrist to help staunch the flow of blood, the other to wrap around the pine cone); tea for the patient, consisting of freshly squeezed lemon, shepherd's purse, nettle, and horsetail; some salt and elder bark in a mojo bag; a small white silk bag with drawstring; parchment for drawing a sigil; a red pen; rose oil; a black altar cloth embroidered with a silver pentagram.

THE RITUAL

The Priestess opens the Circle in the Wicca Way, and invokes the Crone aspect of the goddess.

INVOCATION

"Wise and enduring Lady, you to whom we return when the purposes of our lives are fulfilled, and in whose black, velvety, soundless depths we are nourished and comforted until we are reborn; you who hold sway over the tides of flux and reflux, and who knows the hour of our departures to the inner planes! We trust in your wisdom and awareness to decide when and why we are to be taken from this earth, and what will be the manner of our regeneration. For not only do you take away life, but you also create and nurture it. Ancient Mother, we invoke you to come to us now and enfold us in your mantle of protection, and guide us on this solemn occasion!"

Priestess to the coven: "We gather in this Circle of Inner Light to lend our spiritual strength to ...(the patient) as she terminates the life of the unborn soul within her, and to help the soul on its journey back to the Womb of the Great

Figure 14: Sigil for the Rite on the Occasion of an Abortion

Mother to await rebirth. It is not for us to judge the right or wrong of this act, but rather to ease...(the patient's) recovery from the severe mental, physical, and spiritual trauma she is enduring, and to aid the departed soul's transition back into to the void. Let ...(either the patient, or a spokesperson) communicate to us the details of this affair."

(The spokesperson offers relevant details.)

MEDITATION

Priestess: "Let us consider the theme of tonight's work. As we meditate, I wish you to visualize a ball of light, dull red on the outside, that emits blue and green flashing rays from a pinprick of whirling white light in the center of the ball, where the energy is concentrated. If ever you have witnessed a star nova in space and then collapse upon itself, this is the image I wish you to evoke."

THE RITE

After a time the Priestess brings forth the mojo bag, salt, elder, rose oil, parchment, red pen, and white silk bag.

Priestess: "The salt and the elder are for ... (the patient) to keep by her side as much as possible both before and for forty-eight hours after the operation in order to direct into them her physical and emotional discomfort. When she returns from the hospital, either she, a friend, or a relative will bury the bag in the ground. Salt and elder represent the earth and purification, and are meant to absorb pain and bitterness. The sigil that we now shall draw (figure 14) shows a Pentagram of Solomon inscribed with the Greek word, *oyipa,* which means "wholesome" and "good for the health," and a *tjet,* or buckle of Isis, which instills the wearer with the virtues of the blood of Isis."

The Priestess traces part of the sigil, and hands the parchment around so that each participant can add to it. When the sigil is completed, the Priestess anoints the parchment with rose oil. All begin to chant, *EMOR DIAL HECATEGA* (the Enochian call for the Quarter of Earth). When the chant reaches its apex, the coveners direct the energy into the sigil. The Priestess encloses the sigil in the white silk bag.

Next, the Priestess takes the sigil, tea, and yarn for the patient's wrist and gives them to the patient or her representative. Then she takes the pine cone, symbol of the unborn soul, and the second piece of yarn, and wraps the cone with the yarn, ties it firmly, and lays it in the center of the Circle.

Priestess: "The cone and yarn represent the unborn soul and its tie to this earthly plane. ... (Another covener) shall recite a prayer in order to ease the soul's transition back to the void. Then the Priest shall cut the thread of life."

Covener: "You who are unborn, you who drift in the womb of woman, you who exist in this world, but are not of it. Your destiny is to come among us, but to not appear before us, to exist on this plane for a short while, yet to elude us. Your time to live among us is not yet heralded, and you must return from whence you came to be absorbed again into the void. You do not go, however, without leaving an impression on those of us who have intuited your presence. Nothing is forgotten. The time will come again when you will choose to be reborn into this plane. Then you will walk these mundane paths, and you will know the smell of the forest after the rain, the music of birds in the trees, the green grass and blue sky, and the caress of a breeze on your cheek. One day you will know life. Depart now to the Great Womb in perfect love and perfect peace. Blessed Be!"

After the Priest cuts the thread, the participants sit for a few minutes and visualize sending back the soul to the void, encased in a protective ball of radiant violet light. The Priestess banishes the Circle in the Wicca Way. Then the coven goes outside, and buries the cone and yarn, symbolically returning the soul to Mother Earth.

Ritual to Annihilate a Cancerous Growth

Health spells are tricky operations. In the first place, you should never undertake a healing unless you are in good health yourself and have become magically proficient enough not to absorb the disease into your own body. In order not to retain any of the disease, it is absolutely necessary that while you visualize building a cone of power and light, the energy you draw from the cosmos enters your body and passes through it to the object of the healing. You are merely a conductor of the healing light, and your job is to transmit this energy to the one to be healed. You absorb no energy yourself, nor any of the disease. To be sure that you have rid yourself of the energy and also of any vestiges of the disease you may have inadvertently absorbed, shake out your hands in a direction away from the center of the Circle after you perform the healing operation.

Also, never undertake a healing rite in lieu of a visit to the doctor. Modern medicine would not have been invented if it did not have its place in our society. In general, psychic healing is meant to work hand in hand with standard medical practices—not replace them. Psychic healing also can be effective when, and only when, conventional treatment has failed. Please bear in mind these cautions as you attempt the following healing rite.

ITEMS REQUIRED
Blue altar candles anointed with frankincense oil; Helios incense; matches; coal; holy healing water (which includes water, white vinegar, rosemary, verbena, marjoram, salt, and blue food coloring); parchment for the sigil and blue pen; charm bag; curative herbs (including coriander, eucalyptus, chamomile, buckthorn, yerba santa, life everlasting, basil, and elder); Solomon's seal as an offertory herb; a sapphire stone or other blue stone, clear crystal, coral, jasper, turquoise, or garnet); Wings of Healing anointing oil.

THE RITE
The Priestess opens the Circle using the Wicca Way. Another covener rings the Circle with Solomon's Seal and returns the bowl to altar.

INVOCATION OF RAPHAEL
Priestess: "Raphael of the yellow, orange and blue raiments, Guardian of the Eastern Quarter of the universe, you who preside over new projects and beginnings from your wind-swept heights, you who infuses our intellects with the wisdom of Spirit, guards our health, and keeps us sound in body and mind, I invoke you to lend your power to our rite!"

ANOINTING
The Priestess anoints the patient's third eye, solar plexus and wrists.

Priestess: "In the name of Raphael, god as healer, I anoint you with this mystic oil, whose virtue is to cast away from you all illness and negativity, and to leave you tranquil, comfortable, and healthy."

RAISING THE CONE OF POWER

The Priestess places the patient in the center of the Circle, and the seated coveners joining hands around her and chant *SHEN-UR* ("Circle of Life"). The group visualizes that they are drawing down from a point in the cosmos a ray of bluish-white light that flows through their bodies and out their hands to encase the patient in a cone of light. When the chant reaches its culmination, the coveners direct into the patient the concentrated force of the healing rays

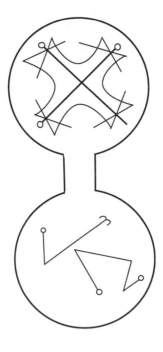

Figure 15: Health Sigil

from the blue-violet end of the astral-light spectrum.

CHARGING THE HEALING HOLY WATER

The Priestess holds her athame over the holy water.

Priestess: "By this sacred blade I cleanse you of evil, negativity and pollution. Be as pure as the whitest snow on the highest mountain top."

The Priestess inserts the point of her athame into the water.

Priestess: "By virtue of my life force I consecrate this water, whose essence is imbued with cleansing, purifying elements. May you work for the health and well-being of ... (the patient). Each time the patient anoints the disease with your healing essence, your potency will spring forth to shrink and destroy the tumor that grows within. Smaller and smaller it withers, wrinkles, and shrivels; little by little, the tumor will dissolve to be carried away by normal bodily processes. So mote it be!"

The Priestess tells the patient to anoint the tumor with holy water every day during the Waning Moon, and at the New Moon to pour on the ground whatever portion remains.

FILLING THE CHARM BAG

One covener draws the sigil (figure 15), another anoints it with Helios oil and encloses it in the bag; another mixes the herbs and places them in the charm bag; yet another anoints the sapphire stone with Wings of Healing oil and drops it in the bag. The Priestess explains to ... (the patient) to carry the bag pinned to the inside of his clothes at his solar plexus until the next Full Moon. Then he must bury the bag or float it down a stream. During the Waning Moon the bag will serve to help rid him of the disease, and during the Waxing Moon it will fill the empty space in his body with healthy cells. The patient sits apart while the coveners chant *CORPUS SANS* ("Healthy Body") over the bag, and direct energy into it.

CLOSING THE CIRCLE

The Priestess closes the Circle using the Wicca Way, and thanks the spirits who have attended the rite. She gives special acknowledgment to the healing angel,

Raphael. The rite is ended. Blessed Be!

Rite of the Chalice of Light

This visualization provides a variation on the Cone of Power segment of the previous ritual. Through imaging techniques you will construct and fill a Chalice of Light in order to reinforce the single group mind and empower it so that the coven may more readily direct energy to the task at hand—in this instance, healing.

Place the patient in the center of the Circle. The coveners sit around the edge of the Circle facing inward, imagining each individual as a separate point of light, love, and energy. After a while, the Priestess rings a bell, lights a white candle as a point of focus, and places it in the Circle. Each covener now envisions the energy of the other coveners as points of light pulsating, glowing, and expanding until they form circles. The circles grow until they merge as one.

When the Priestess rings the bell again, the coveners link hands and envision a thin stream of blue-white light encircling them, forming a chalice. They chant *KE NO SAN MYRRE SAN TE ORLEN* (a channeled coven chant) and cause the chalice to rise above their heads, forming a cone of power.

When the chant reaches its most intense moment, the coveners release each other's hands and train the light from the chalice through their bodies and out their fingertips toward the patient. It helps to rub your hands together briskly before directing the light. When the tingling leaves your hands, sit quietly with your hands in your lap until all have finished.

Uncrossing and Protection Ritual

Perform this ritual when the Moon is waning on a Tuesday in the hour of Mars.

ITEMS REQUIRED

A black altar cloth; a red candle anointed with Dragon's Bane perfume; a black candle anointed with the zodiac oil of the person who bears the petitioner a grudge, or if this is unknown, Hexbreaker oil; rosemary oil for anointing the petitioner; parchment and a red-ink pen to draw the sigil; dragon's blood powder; a mojo bag.

OPENING THE CIRCLE
The Priestess opens the Circle using the Lesser Pentagram Ritual.

INVOCATION TO MAAT
Priestess: "Maat, goddess of the unalterable laws of heaven and daughter of Ra, through whom he lives, you who weighs the purity of our lives against a feather in your balance when we appear before you on Judgment Day, I beseech you to come to our aid in our just war concerning the evil perpetrated against ... (the petitioner). Mighty Maat, come shield us and assist us with your righteous outrage in our struggle."

INVOCATION OF KHAMAEL
Priest: "Khamael, terrible Archangel of Mars and the Seraphim who are the incendiary serpents of our planet; fiery Graphiel, Intelligence of Mars, and Bartzabel and Phalegh, simmering spirits of the red planet, in the name of Elohim Gebur I invoke these potent beings to rally in our defense in the battle against this scourge."

All coveners repeat *KHAMAEL* five times.

The petitioner cuts a pentagram into a red candle with the athame and anoints it, starting in the center and working to the bottom; then center to top. She lights the candle and recites, "Blazing flame, symbol of passion, will, and transmutation; my champion and protector, essence of the Sun that purges everything of filth and decay, deliver me from the bane that besets me." (The petitioner adds a personal description of the difficulty).

The petitioner cuts the initials of the tormentor into the black candle and anoints it, then proclaims: "This candle represents the malfeasance wrought by...(the tormentor)." The petitioner lights the candle. "As this candle burns, let the evil incinerate. May the injury wrought by ... (the tormentor) be deflected from me and returned to the sender!"

All shout five times: "So mote it be!"

Petitioner: "As this candle burns, so may the evil, negativity and

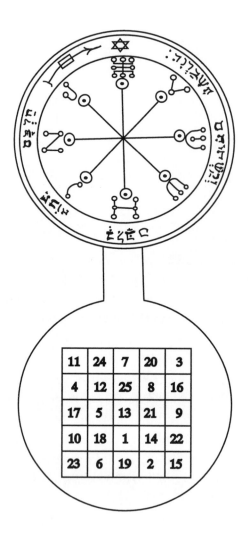

Figure 16: Hexbreaker Sigil

imbalance instigated against me by ... be dissipated. May the evil return to the sender. Let harmony again prevail!"

All repeat five times: "By the power of Khamael, so mote it be!"

The Priestess anoints the petitioner on the third eye and on each shoulder with rosemary oil.

Priestess: "In the power of Maat, I anoint you so that you may be free of the harm that has befallen you. May your mind be free, may your heart be free, may your body be free."

The coveners take turns tracing parts of the sigil until it is complete (figure 16). The petitioner may also trace her name on the magic square if she so desires. The petitioner anoints the seal and places it in the mojo bag with dragons' blood powder, then puts the bag in the center of the Circle. The coveners raise a cone of power over the bag with the chant, *"SEM."* At the proper moment, they direct the power of the Universal Light into the bag.

The Priestess closes the Circle with the Lesser Banishing Pentagram Ritual.

Rite of Power and Influence Over Another

It is not considered morally correct within the Law of Wicca to attempt to control another's mind. Witches believe that all people are equal entities with the same rights, and that they all have specific purposes for being incarnated on this planet. The laws of Karma are complex, and your Higher Self may decide to put a difficult person or situation in your way to test your response.

However, situations exist where one person clearly obstructs the path of another, and continued obstruction could be harmful, or even deadly. In these instances, I believe it is proper to perform a ritual where the afflicted person endeavors to influence the opinions of the obstructor to "see the light;" that is, exercise reason when dealing with the problem in order to reach a more just conclusion. In such a ritual, you should never attempt to change the obstructor's nature. The aim should be a clearer, truer understanding of the issue, and a release of the stranglehold on the petitioner's life.

ITEMS REQUIRED

Purification bath salts; a candle of your astral color anointed with your zodiac oil; two white altar candles anointed with Spirit oil; one purple candle anointed with High John the Conqueror oil; one black candle anointed with Hexbreaker oil; one orange candle, anointed with Merlin's Magic oil; dragon's blood powder; salt and water; a piece of netting spray-painted silver, Compelling incense, to which you must add frankincense and myrrh pieces; coal, incense burner, matches; a black altar cloth bordered with white.

Erect your altar as in the configuration shown below. Go to the obstructor's house or workplace, and on the doorstep make a Qabalistic Cross enclosed in a circle (figure 17) with dragon's blood powder. Return home, and take a purification bath, using the salts. Go to your altar, light the white altar candles, and perform the Middle Pillar Ritual. Meditate on the obstructor and the obstacle(s) she has put in your path. Visualize her having a change of mind.

Altar

white altar candle		white altar candle
your astral candle	purple power candle	black obstruction candle
	orange attraction candle	
incense burner		copy of the ritual

INVOCATION OF THE LORD TO THE UNIVERSE

When you have finished your meditation, light the incense and imagine that all the power of the element Air is rising from the smoke. Recite:

"Omnipotent Lord of the Universe, you whose luminescence sparks all life, you whose roaring might blows more dreadfully than the most surly sea! Oh faceless, timeless One, I invoke you to come and dwell in my heart and aid me in my time of need!"

INVOCATION TO BINAH

"Mother of dark shapes, queen of mystery, unerring justice and strength of severity; you who are known as Binah, High Priestess of the Concealed Silver

Star; come, gather your legions of dreadful furies around me and aid me in my hour of darkness. Be unto me the light that shines for me deep within the black cavern."

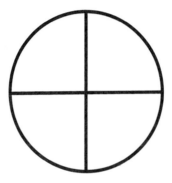

Figure 17: Qabalistic Cross Enclosed in a Circle

CANDLE MAGIC

Take your astral candle and hold it in both your hands for a few minutes. Feel the candle warm in your hand, then carve your initials in it and return it to its holder. Say:

"Here stand I, an unassailable castle, a tower of power. My invulnerability conquers all. My image is reflected in this candle (light candle), which distills the essence of wisdom, knowledge, strength, and superiority. My irreproachable qualities are recognized by all."

Light the purple candle. "This candle symbolizes my power that is pure and sincere in its intentions. In the eyes of the world I am unqualifiedly worthy of my goal that until now has been blocked." (Add a personal description of what you want to achieve and why you are thwarted.)

Take the black candle in your hand, and hold it until it warms. Carve the initials of the obstructor into the candle, (or if it is a matter of simply an impossible situation rather than a person, carve in a keyword that describes the difficulty), sprinkle it with saltwater, and return it to its holder. Recite:

"Blessed be this waxen figure. By human hands you are made, by human will you are changed. No longer are you wax, but flesh and blood. I name you ... (the obstructor), the obstacle to my plans. *(Light the candle.)* What a puny, charred, and wizened figure you are! You are insecure in your sense of self and purpose, and so you run hither and thither in need of someone to dominate. Yet you will never dominate me!"

"All knowledge of *YHVH* (Yod Hay Vau Hay) be to me!

All strength of *ADNI* (Adonai) be to me!

All love of *EHEIH* (Ay Hay Yeh) be to me!"

Light the orange candle. "As this candle flares, so the irresistible attraction of my will blazes forth in its indomitable glory. My enemy is enchanted by its glow. She cannot take away her eyes. Soon she drifts under the hypnotic sway of my mastery and accedes to my desire.

"Everybody favors me. Everybody opposes ... (the obstructor). The cold fish is out of water, and is confused. She turns everywhere for guidance, but no familiar terrain appears. She gulps at the air for nourishment, but chokes on every breath. The eyes bulge, and the chest seems as if it will burst.

"Nonetheless, all the pain and confusion will vanish as soon as she grants me my desire, and removes the obstacle(s) from my path."

Extinguish the black candle, and drop the silver net over it, binding it so tightly around the candle that the obstructor will never again be able to harm others as she has tried to harm you. Proclaim:

"By air, earth, water and fire, so be you bound, as I desire. By three and nine, your power I bind. By Moon and Sun, my will be done. Sky and sea keep harm from me. As the cord goes `round, your power is bound. Light revealed, now be sealed! You will (state your wish) now!"

Close the Temple in the usual manner, and thank the spirits who have helped you. Extinguish the altar candles; let the others burn down. After cleaning the ritual space, go outside and dig a hole in the garden to bury the black, netted candle; float it down a stream; or place it in a box and hide it in a dark place until your wish is granted. Then destroy the candle and bury the remains. Recite a short prayer of thanksgiving to Binah and the Lord of the Universe for granting your wish.

Spell for Attraction

For the years I have owned and operated my mail-order metaphysical supplies business, WildWood Studio, probably the most frequent request I receive is for spells, talismans, stones, herbs, etc., to promote love. The need for love can take many forms, from physical desire to marriage, regaining a love lost, keeping a partner faithful, etc. Here I suggest to you how to find a new love. This spell can be performed equally effectively by males as by females of all ages.

PRELIMINARIES

If you wish to attract a lover, but have no one special in mind, you may find yourself faced with a seemingly insurmountable task. By using the appropriate herbs and oils at the right time, you both concentrate your thoughts and focus completely on your intention to link your will with the love aspect of the Universal Mind. You tap into the "amatory energy" that flows through the cosmos. The items you use have been employed successfully over centuries to bring love into peoples' lives. Because they contain attraction vibrations in their essences, and also because people have believed in them for so long, they have accumulated a considerable amount of power.

Although I suggest specific herbs and oils in the spell that follows, you may substitute any of the oils on the following list.

OILS

almond—attraction
amber—faithfulness

ambergris—sexual desire
anise—offering to Macumba goddess of love
camphor—brings quick results
civet—love
clove—seduction
clover—faithfulness
cyclamen—enduring love
frangipani—attraction
ginger—livens up a relationship
ginger blossom—stimulation
honey—enchantment, enticement
hyacinth—attraction
jasmine—attraction
lotus—attraction
musk—attraction, passion
rose—love, peace
sweet pea—attracts love from strangers
tuberose—to be used exclusively by males
vanilla—powerful attraction
ylang-ylang—seduction

HERBS
aloes (the wood, not aloe vera); basil; clove; coriander; damiana; dill; elecampane; endive; ginseng (both root and powder); kava kava; lovage; marjoram; musk crystals; nutmeg; sea holly.

LOVE DUST
Before you go out in search of somebody new, mix a batch of love dust.
Ingredients:
1 cup dried, crushed red and pink rose petals
2 tablespoons musk crystals
1 tablespoon vanilla crystals

1/4 cup dried, crushed peppermint leaves

1/4 cup dried chamomile flowers

Crush the ingredients in a mortar and pestle, and add:

2 teaspoons rose oil

2 teaspoons musk oil

7 drops peppermint oil.

Mix thoroughly. Activate the dust by holding your index finger and second finger (or athame) over the powder, and declare: "By the power of Ishtar, Erzulie, Maria Padilha, Venus, and Aphrodite, I charge this potion to bring the right man (or woman) into my life. May he be attracted to me like a magnet."

Rub some of the powder on your hands before going out. Also before leaving home, take an attraction bath to which you have added 1/2 teaspoon clove oil and 3 teaspoons jasmine oil. Add a sprinkling of dill seeds to the bath.

Or you may want to try this Macumba (Brazilian neo-African religion) bath, which I translate from the Portuguese.

ATTRACTION BATH

Ingredients:

hollyhock leaves; eucalyptus; cologne; white carnation; white rose petals.

Preparation:

Boil all the ingredients for twenty minutes, and strain. Pour the mixture over your body, and let it trickle down without drying it off. Take this bath before you go to sleep or leave the house." [28]

THE SPELL

Perform this spell once a day for seven days, ending on a Friday as close to the full Moon as possible. Work the Magic at dawn every day except for the last day when you can do the rite either at dawn or between one and three o'clock in the afternoon.

Gather together the following ingredients: Erzulie perfume oil (3 parts rose, 1 part jasmine, 1/2 part vanilla, 1/2 part frangipani); seven love pellets (mix brown sugar and butter with ground hazelnuts and a dash of ginger and cinnamon powders); a two-foot length of red yarn; parchment paper cut into a circle and a red pen; a red mojo bag; American or Mexican turquoise (most turquoise sold these days comes from Asia, and is inferior in quality; so ask your vendor); a small bowl in which to mix equal parts coriander, lovage, marjoram, dried pulverized endive, damiana, kava kava, and elecampane; magnetic sand; Compelling perfume (3 parts musk, 1 part lotus, 7 drops ginger blossom).

On the first day you perform the ritual, open the Circle using the Wicca Way and perform the Middle Pillar ritual. Eat one of the pellets and for a few minutes try to visualize the person you will meet. Is she tall, short, thin, fat, dark, light? What is her age? eye color? type of clothes?

Now tie a knot in the center of the yarn. As you do so, recite:

"With this knot I bind you to me on the physical plane. May you be attracted to me immediately, and be consumed with the desire to know me better. In the name of Erzulie (sprinkle a drop of Erzulie on the knot), I demand this physically manifest."

Enclose the yarn in a mojo bag and place it under your pillow until the next day. Close the Circle and banish all spirits as usual.

Repeat this ritual each day for five more days, each time tying a knot, first to the left, then to the right of the central knot, one or two inches apart. As you tie each knot, focus on a different aspect of the love you wish to draw, and recite the following:

Day 2: "With this knot I bind you to me sexually. May you burn with passion to possess me and be fulfilled with me as I will be with you. In the name of Erzulie, I demand this physically manifest."

Day 3: "With this knot I bind you to me mentally. May our intellects pulsate in harmony, and may we each learn from each other's complementary natures. In the name of Erzulie, I demand this physically manifest!"

Day 4: "With this knot I bind you to me emotionally. May our sensitivities mingle happily and serve as sympathetic supports for each other. In the name of Erzulie, I demand this physically manifest!"

Day 5: "With this knot I bind you to me spiritually. May our spirits vibrate together harmoniously on the higher planes. In the name of Erzulie, I demand this physically manifest!"

Day 6: "With this knot I draw your soul to mine. May we discover the true meaning of the words 'soul mate' and fulfill our destinies together. In the name of Erzulie, I demand this physically manifest!"

On the seventh day, gather together the other ingredients outlined at the beginning of this spell. After eating the pellets, anoint the base of your neck, behind the ears, breasts, and back of knees with Compelling perfume. Draw the seal of Erzulie, goddess of love, on the seal (figure 18), and anoint the edges with Erzulie oil. Tie the seventh knot. Tie both ends of the yarn together in a knot, and anoint both knots with Erzulie oil. Then lay the yarn on top of the seal. Cup your hands over the yarn and seal (without touching them) and invoke Erzulie:

"Lithe and lovely goddess, Erzulie, surround me and my talisman in a mist of rose and emerald light. Bring the object of my desire to me so that I may receive the joy of love and emanate love in return."

Place the yarn and seal in the mojo bag, anoint the turquoise with Compelling perfume, and pray:

"May my wish rise to the heavens through this sky-colored stone and be granted very soon."

Place the turquoise, herbs, and magnetic sand into the bag; seal it. Pin it to the inside of your clothing as close to your heart as possible, and wear it until you find your new love.

Close the Circle in the usual manner. After you meet your love, perform this rite of thanksgiving to Erzulie.

Go to a quiet corner of a park, forest, or your own back yard. Open a Circle and call to Erzulie:

"Dew Lady of the shimmering rose and emerald light, I thank you for granting my wish and conferring the joys of love upon me. As a token of my esteem I offer you these roses (toss three bright red roses on the ground, and encircle them with dragons' blood powder). *Evoe Erzulie!*"

Close the Circle in the usual manner. Keep the talismanic bag in your underwear drawer and anoint it weekly with rose oil to keep your love true. May the goddess shine her infinite love on you!

MACUMBA RITUAL OF ATTRACTION

When I lived in Rio de Janeiro, I was involved with the popular neo-African religion practiced there called Macumba. Although Macumba chooses other ways than Wicca does to contact the cosmic forces, those who practice these neo-African/

Figure 18: Seal of Freda

European/Indian rites are searching for the same unity with the godhead as we are. As I studied the unique religious and philosophical system of Macumba, I grew to respect the *macumbeiros* —as the practitioners of this faith call themselves—their methods, and their goals. I believe that followers of various spiritual paths have much to learn from each other. Therefore, I include here a Macumba love ritual for your edification and enjoyment by Texeira Alves Neto. The ritual calls upon the help of the Pomba-Gira Arripiada, a female goddess, who according to Macumba philosophy, specializes in helping mortals with affairs of the heart. The translated text follows.

Among the thousands of other Pombas-Giras. Arripiada specializes in listening to requests for money and love. She is endowed with great kindness and extraordinary power.

Like all the other Pombas-Giras, Arripiada likes flowers, particularly red roses, and therefore, any 'offering' or 'present' to her, whether or not it is a 'promise,' should contain, among other things, red roses. Her colors clearly are red and black.

Her '"dwelling place,"' is a 'T' crossroad, that is, the spot where one street empties into another, without, however, crossing it.

Whenever you want to ask a favor of the Pomba-Gira Arripiada, you should proceed in the following manner:

At the crossroads itself, and not in the middle of the street that flows into the other, begin by greeting the Pomba-Gira in more or less the following manner:

'Salve a Pomba-Gira Arripiada! Salve a sua encruzilhada!'

('Hail to the Pomba-Gira, Arripiada! Hail to your crossroad!')

Once you have done this, spread out on the ground a red silk cloth or paper, and on top of it place a black one. Next, on top of these pieces of cloth or paper, place a bunch of seven bright red roses tied together with a black ribbon. Light a black and red candle which you have placed one on each side of the cloths.

After you have made all these offerings to Pomba-Gira Arripiada, say the following:

'You are famous for your work, for your kindness and for your great strength and power. I beseech you, Pomba-Gira Arripiada, to resolve the following situation (or the following problem) for me ... I know, my Lady, that your force and power are great and that, greater yet is my faith in your work. Therefore, I await with faith and patience for you to take up my case and find the solution to my situation.'[29]

Past-Life Recall: The Black Singing Waters of the Great Mother

As you already have learned, belief in reincarnation forms a part of Craft doctrine. We find it useful to recall certain past lives in order to elicit the knowledge gained during these lives to help both ourselves and others in this incarnation. The reason why I teach my students past-life recall after initiation is that I find that by then students have acquired enough Craft maturity not to abuse the method. By abuse, I mean that unless one takes the proper attitude toward delving into past lives, the process can be overwhelming. I have seen people, who when introduced to past-life recall too early, indulged in it to the exclusion of all other Wicca study. Admittedly, it is thrilling to explore the vivid worlds of one's past lives. Nevertheless, the experience must be viewed in the right perspective. To let its fascination grab hold of you and supersede your present life can diminish and even destroy the patterns you have set for yourself in this lifetime.

Past-life recall is one tool for the attainment of increased self-knowledge and self-improvement. You can access information collected in your previous lives, which may include anything from herbal lore to ancient Tibetan invocations long ago forgotten. But this is only one way to acquire higher knowledge, and it can never replace the benefits gained through meditation, ritual, reading, helping others, and plain, hard work.

With this admonition in mind, I shall teach you the past-life recall technique known as "The Black Singing Waters" that I learned from my Priestess, Maaisa.

Ideally, another initiate, preferably your Priestess, should take you through the waters on the first few occasions. However, it is possible to do it for yourself. For this rite you will need a smooth nugget of absolutely black obsidian (the commonly found snowflake obsidian won't do), four white candles, Astral Projection incense, several blankets, a pillow, and hot tea, coffee, or juice. Sometimes, on emerging from the Waters, people can suddenly be overcome by a paralyzing chill. If this should happen to you, wrap up well in the blankets and sip the hot liquid offered you by the other participants until you warm up.

Brew the drink and let it simmer while you perform the ritual. Place the blankets in a location where you can grab them easily as soon as the rite is over. Dress simply in a black robe, and remove all leather and jewelry. You need not erect an altar, but you will require enough room so you can stretch out on your back on the floor. Place two candles near where your feet will be and two beyond where your shoulders will lie. Put the pillow where you will lay your head.

Light the candles and incense, and perform the Lesser Banishing Pentagram Ritual. Lie down on your back, make yourself comfortable, and place the obsidian nugget on your third eye. The obsidian opens the door to the Black Singing Waters.

Begin to put yourself through a kind of auto-hypnosis. First, tense your muscles. After a moment relax them one group at a time. Beginning with your forehead and move to your eyes, nose, cheeks, mouth, neck, shoulders, and so forth until you finish at your toes. Empty your mind, as you have been taught to do in meditation, and perform rhythmic breathing exercises if this helps you to relax.

After you are thoroughly relaxed, have repeated to you or repeat to yourself the phrases in the next several paragraphs, aloud if necessary, to maintain concentration. (If you perform the rite solo, change the second person "you" to the first person "I.")

"You are relaxed now, completely relaxed. All the cares of the day have dissolved from the corners of your mind, and you feel peaceful and tranquil, but refreshed and alert. Your muscles are loose, your body is relaxed, your mind is at rest. Completely relaxed, completely at ease.

"You feel weightless, as light as a feather floating, floating calmly in the air. The air around you is warm and dark, comfortable and comforting. And you are moving through the warming darkness without effort. Warming darkness. Floating calmly and effortlessly in the Black Singing Waters, the Womb of the Great Mother. The Womb is dark, the womb is warm. The Womb is boundless, and you realize you have been here, boundless before. You feel at home, protected and nurtured in your journey through the Boundless Black Waters.

"As you swim through these dark, silent, familiar waters, you notice a pinpoint of light ahead of you, as if at the end of a long, long tunnel. The light is just an insignificant speck, but it interests you mildly, and you decide to draw nearer to it.

"Gradually the area of light becomes larger—oh so gradually. It increases and enlarges and takes up more and more of the darkness. You are approaching nearer and nearer, nearer to the light. Nearer and nearer, higher and higher. The light is now a large white brilliance about the size of a doorway, and you can pass through.

"As you move through the doorway, you find yourself in a new place, and for the first time you are cognizant of your body. You glance down at your feet. What are you wearing on your feet? Look at your arm. How are you clothed? Are you wearing any ornaments? What do your hands look like? To what kind of person do they belong?

"Now look about at the landscape. What do you see? Are you indoors or outdoors? Are there any people moving about? What do they look like? What are they doing? What is the season? Do you know where you are? Can you identify the epoch? What age are you? What is your station in life? What do you do for a living? Are you a male or female? Do you have any relatives? What is your state of mind? Are you happy? Sad? Angry? Why have you returned to this lifetime? What is the significance of this life? Do you have any information to bring into your current life to help yourself or others? Any messages for us?

"You find the scene before your eyes grow hazy, and you know it is time to leave. You begin to withdraw into the darkness, and the light recedes. Slowly, every so slowly, you turn and swim back into the darkness through the Womb of the Great Mother. Through the Black Singing Waters of the Great Mother. And the darkness is soothing and comforting. It is an all-healing blackness-blankness, and you float onward through its restorative waters. Dark, singing waters. Waters that caress you.

"Onward you float and now upward, ever so slowly and smoothly, slowly and smoothly, until you find that the tip of your nose is emerging, then your face, head, hair, shoulders, and the rest of your body. At last you fully emerge into this time and this place, here and now, in this incarnation."

If crossing the barrier between the worlds has made you feel cold, this is a normal condition. Remove the obsidian from your forehead, stand up, turn on the lights, wrap yourself in blankets, and drink the hot liquid. If someone else has led you through the Waters this person will have written in a notebook or used a tape recorder to record what you said while in the Waters. You may remember additional impressions that you did not speak aloud during the You may be excited about your experience, and dream of it later in the week. Be sure to write down all impressions that occur to you, or that you receive from dreams. Enjoy the Black Singing Waters, but remember not to overindulge.

Chapter Six
Trees

In order to perform Tree Magic effectively it is best to understand something about these enchanting large botanicals. Trees usually live for several years and form, or try to form, a central woody stem. Their circulatory systems, through which they move sap, are analogous to the blood pressure mechanism in humans. Measurable movements within include respiration, spasms, and electrical impulses. Incredibly, trees have been anesthetized with chloroform in order to transplant them with a minimum of shock to their systems. Indeed, trees are living, breathing entities.

At one time most of Europe and North and South America were covered with dense forests out of which early tribes made clearings in order to plant crops. Trees in themselves are superior sources of food, shelter, weapons, and other necessities, and our ancestors soon began to worship the tree spirits that they imagined inhabited these towering timbers. They were convinced that trees conferred fertility on crops and humans; consequently, they originated many interesting customs and rites centered around these beliefs.

Later, they generalized their worship from spirits of individual trees to forest deities who represented all the trees. The Druids carried their reverence of trees so far as to abide in sacred groves. Remnants of this custom persisted into recent history: in colonial times, Christian ministers would deliver sermons from beneath oak and ash trees.

Our ancestors were correct not to underestimate the importance of trees. Because trees need carbon dioxide in order to synthesize food, they cleanse the air of pollutants. As part of the synthesizing process, they release oxygen into the air that people need in order to breathe.

Trees also absorb ground water, which when re-released into the atmosphere eventually falls as rain. For example, a large eucalyptus tree will disgorge eighty-two gallons of water into the air over a twenty-four hour period. Trees capture, protect, and fertilize topsoil, give shelter to birds that eat insect pests, and provide people with products for furniture, paper, dyes, weapons, medicine, and nourishment.

As the highest form of vegetable consciousness, trees are considered guardians of this planet. Dorothy MacLean and founders of the experimental farm and spiritual center at Findhorn, Scotland, conducted experiments to contact spirits known as dryads, who supposedly inhabit the woods. Based on the results of these experiments, MacLean firmly believes that large trees act as channels of universal forces of strength, stability, and continuity. She holds that trees send messages to humans about our well being and the welfare of this planet. She concludes that it is our duty to protect trees in return for the good they do for us.

Witches use trees to make power wands, broomsticks, staffs, needfire mix, incense, and anointing oils. We revitalize ourselves by tapping into tree energy, interpret tree vibrations in order to divine the past, present and future, and include the Druidic tree alphabet and its esoteric meanings in our philosophical system. We use the medicinal properties of trees as well as those of other plants in order to heal ourselves. The tree reference in the appendix at the end of this book will help you plan meditations and rituals that center around trees.

Any time you cut a part from a tree, explain to the tree why you need what it has to offer, ask its permission to cut it, and leave an offering of water or wine at the base of the trunk. If you collect wood for needfire mix, use dead wood, leaves, and fruit that have already fallen from the tree.

The Tree Alphabet

The Tree Alphabet is a magical system of divination devised by the Druids. The thirteen consonants take their names from trees native to Great Britain. Thirteen trees were chosen because they correspond to the thirteen lunar months. Each tree incorporates philosophical concepts expressed in the seasonal rituals of the Druids' religion. Usually the trees are in flower at the time of year over which they hold sovereignty. Learn the tree alphabet and incorporate its rich symbolism into your rituals. Whenever you perform Tree Magic, refer to the following calendar to broaden your arborital knowledge.

Name	Tree	Letter	Month	Deity
Beth	Birch	B	Dec. 24-Jan. 20	Ceridwen
Luis	Rowan	L	Jan 21-Feb. 17	Brigit
Nion	Ash	N	Feb. 18-Mar. 17	Gwydion
Fearn	Alder	F	Mar. 18-Apr.14	Bran
Saille	Willow	S	Apr. 15-May 12	Arianhod
Uath	Hawthorn	H	May 13-Jun. 9	Olwen
Duir	Oak	D	Jun. 10-Jul. 7	Lugh, the Dagda
Tinne	Holly, Holly Oak	T	Jul. 8-Aug. 4	Cuchulain
Cill	Hazel	C	Aug. 5-Sept. 1	Mannanan
Muin	Vine	M	Sept. 2-Sept. 29	Sadv
Gort	Ivy	G	Sept. 30-Oct. 27	Palu
Peith	Dwarf Elder	B	Oct. 28-Nov. 24	Gwyn
Ngetal	Reed	NG		
Ruis	Elder	R	Nov.25-Dec. 22	Cailleach

December 23 is an extra day excluded from the original tree calendar, although it is now incorporated into the first month of the Druidic year. It is dedicated to the *oll-lach,* or mistletoe, most revered of plants, and is the day set aside to prepare for the arrival of the Child of Light; that is, the new year. In the *Song of Amerigin,* an old Irish poem that explores the calendar theme, it is said cryptically of that day, "Who but I knows the secrets of the unhewn dolmen?"

Phrases from the *Song of Amergin* and versions of the poem found in *The Book of Leacon* and the *Book of the O'Clerys,* and another explanation from the *Romance of Taliesin,* reprinted and interpreted by Robert Graves in *The White Goddess,* provide clues into the esoteric meanings of the original consonants as follows:

B = I am a stag of seven tines. I am an ox in strength. I
have been a fierce bull and a yellow bird (strength, birth).
L = I am a wide flood in a plain. I am a flood in a plain.
I have been a boat on the sea (magic, extent).
N = I am a wind in the deep waters. I am a wind on the sea.
I fled vehemently on the foam of water (depth).
F = I am a shining tear of the Sun. I am a ray of the Sun.
I have been a drop in the air (strength, purity).
S = I am a hawk on a cliff. I am a bird of prey on a cliff. I
journeyed as an eagle (cunning, enchantment).
H = I am fair among flowers. I am a shrewd navigator. God
made me of blossom (meaning unclear, but the month is
associated with fertility).
D = I am a god who sets the head afire with smoke. I am god in
the power of transformation. I have been a tree stump in a shovel (poetry).
T = I am a battle wagon, or spear. I am a giant with a sharp
sword hewing down an army. I fled as a spearhead of woe
to such as wish for woe (vengeance).
C = I am a salmon in the pool. I have been a blue salmon
(wisdom).
M = I am a hill of poetry. I am a skilled artist. I have been a

spotted snake on a hill (exaltation).

G = I am a ruthless boar. I am a fierce boar. I fed as a
bristly boar seen in a ravine (valor).

NG = I am a threatening noise of the sea. I am the roaring of the sea. I have
been a wave breaking on the beach (terror, death).

R = I am a wave of the sea. On a boundless sea I was set
adrift (rebirth).[30]

There are also tree correspondences for the five vowels. However, since the thirteen months are already occupied by the consonants, the vowels and their tree associations refer to seasons, or important Druidic calendar dates in the following:

Name	Tree	Vowel	Season
Ailm	Silver Fir	A	December 24
Eahda	Aspen	E	Autumn Equinox
Idho	Yew	I	December 22
Ohn	Furze	O	Spring Equinox
Ura	Heather	U	Summer Solstice

In addition to the vowels and consonants, two other letters carry tree associations. The letter Q (Quertz), because it was written often as *CC* in Old Irish manuscripts, and Z (Straif), written as *SS,* belong to the months of Coll and Saille. Their respective trees are apple or hazel, and blackthorn or willow.

Needfire Mix

A combination of nine of almost any number of sacred woods composes the Sabbat needfire mix. Witches place the needfire in the pot, light it, and dance around it, occasionally leaping over the cauldron. When Witches leap the cauldron at Hallowmas it is to show that they leave behind the cares and woes of the old year. When we leap at the Winter Solstice we welcome in the new year. Often we burn sacred herbs as petitions to the Lord and Lady in the needfire flames. Refer to chapter 4 to see how to incorporate the Rite of the Needfire into seasonal rituals.

To prepare needfire mix, collect (the best time is on the Summer Solstice) nine sacred woods. The wood can come from any tree as long as it is not elder, yew or willow, which carry negative associations as far as needfire mix is concerned. Trees possess many positive associations that you can use according to the intent of your ritual. The usual woods include: oak, pine, spruce, ash, birch, rowan, hawthorn, cedar, fir, and hazel. Cherry is one of the preferred sacred woods, but be sure to renew your supply frequently as this wood spoils quickly. Experiment with other woods tailored to the needs of specific rituals. For example, mix in holly for the winter rites, and fern and furze (gorse) at Hallowmas. Apple is superb for Fertility Magic or summer rites. See the appendix for a more complete list of the meanings of trees.

Chop bits of branches and bark small enough not to create a major conflagration in your cauldron. I add bits of bark, resin, leaves, moss, nuts, and small dried fruit. I like to incorporate cedar in the form of powder or granules, and steep the mixture in a small amount of fragrant oil for a few weeks, turning it each day so that it matures. Cedar granules help adhere the mixture , while the oils, besides adding a delightful fragrance, help the needfire ignite when lighted. My favorite needfire oil is rose, which holds great symbolic value. On certain occasions I vary the recipe. For example, at Hallowmas I may choose narcissus, dark musk, and a hint of patchouli. At the Winter Solstice I may combine spruce, fir, redwood, and pine oils.

Tree Magic

To cure someone of an illness that is not so severe that it prevents walking, take the patient to a tall, straight coconut, fig, lime, oak, pine, palm, or walnut tree. Carry along at least a gallon of water into which you have mixed a cup of mead and one-half cup honey. Approach the tree, and at about twenty yards, salute it with your elbows bent and forearms raised to your head level, palms facing outward. Call the salutation, *Salve* (pronounced "Sahlvee").

As you draw closer to the tree, explain to it why you need its assistance, and ask it to remove the disease from the patient and ground it.

Have the patient sit down with back against the tree. The person will sit more comfortably on a pillow, but nothing should come between the patient's back and the tree trunk. As the subject relaxes, measure a length of red yarn to encircle both patient and tree, with enough length remaining to tie three knots and the string together at the back of the tree. Dig a small hole at the back of the tree. Next, perform the following knot spell with the yarn. As you tie each knot, say:

"May ... (the patient's) illness be held fast in these knots, never to escape these bonds *(tie the first knot),* but to be grounded in the Mother Earth *(tie the second knot).* May ... be cured of ... (the illness) *(tie the third knot),* which will remain imprisoned here forever."

Wrap the yarn around the patient and the tree, and tie it at the back of the tree. Meditate for fifteen minutes, visualizing the illness absorbed by the tree's energy and earthed to the ground. Then untie the yarn, put it in a mojo bag, and bury it in the hole. Both you and the subject then stand and thank the tree for lending its energy to the rite. As a token of gratitude, pour a libation of water, honey, and mead in front of the trunk, and walk away.

Soul Tree

You may wish to consecrate a soul tree, which is a personal tree that will grow with you as you mature in body, mind, and spirit, and with which you can share your most intimate thoughts. Choose a tree that seems to fit your character. The following are particularly positive: hazel, ash, mountain ash, pine, fir, rosemary, oak, linden, apple. Pot a tree seedling, or buy a small pre-potted tree. These are available from most nurseries and gardening centers in the spring and fall. If you do not want to plant the tree outside (if you think you may move away or do not have a garden or access to the countryside), choose a Norfolk Pine or a palm tree, because they do well indoors and can travel with you.

Water and care for your tree in the usual fashion until the Winter Solstice. On that Sabbat, take the potted tree to the ritual. On a piece of parchment ,write the name you have chosen for the tree in red ink and attach it with red thread

188188 Web of Light

to a branch.

During the ritual set aside a segment of time during which you name the tree, declare it as your soul tree, and ask that the blessings of the Lord and Lady be conferred upon it. Water it with the consecrated water from the western Quarter. (See chapter 3 for more details.)

If it is an indoor tree, keep it inside, and be sure it receives enough light and moisture. If you plant the tree outside, wait until the Spring Equinox, and include a tree planting ceremony as part of the proceedings.

If you prefer an already established tree, go to a large tree of the kind I mentioned, and salute it in the manner prescribed in the tree health spell. Tell the tree your name, and ask if it will consent to be your tree guardian. Then communicate to it the name you have selected for it. Take one of its fruits (nut, cone, berry, etc.), anoint it with Cernunnos oil, and place it in a crevice or where two branches meet, as a symbol of the bond between you. Wrap your arms around the tree and give it a good squeeze, full of love. Go to the tree whenever you wish to be revitalized, meditate, or just talk. Bring it a libation from time to time and keep it trimmed of dead leaves and branches. At the Winter Solstice and Summer Solstice decorate your tree guardian with colorful strips of cloth.

Appendix
The Meaning of Trees

Acacia
Scientific Name: genus *Acacia*
Common Names: Sweet Acacia; Mimosa; Gum Arabic; Wattle Bark (Australia); Koa Wood (Hawaii).
Deities: Kether (the creator god); Diana; Osiris; Tree of Life.
Uses: Furniture-making, leather tanning, cosmetics. Gum arabic (*A. senegal*), made by boiling the resin in water, is an adhesive and scents pomanders, sachets, and solar incense. Acacia alleviates catarrh, coughs, diarrhea, typhus, and dysentery. The astringent tree bark cures inflammations. Also use to aid digestive or urinary problems.
Magical Lore: Make acacia wands for General Magic. Add gum arabic to incense to attract good fortune and friendly spirits, and to stimulate the psychic centers. Burn the flowers as an offering in love petitions. Isis is said to have sailed around the world in a boat made from acacia wood in search of her lover, Osiris.

Alder
Scientific Name: *Alnus glutinosa*
Deities: Astarte; Bran; Venus
Uses: The leaves spread in corners of the room eliminate fleas and flies, and the inner bark mixed with vinegar kills lice. Drink the bark as a tea to cure skin problems. Distill the leaves in water and apply topically to lessen inflammation and swelling.

Early Europeans built their houses at the banks of lakes on alder piles because the wood resists rot. Beautiful furniture is carved from the wood in Scotland, and so it is sometimes called Scottish mahogany.

Magical Lore: Alder fought in the front line in the Irish battle of the trees. It is called the "fire tree" because it bleeds red when cut, and therefore, is sacred to Bran, the fire god. Witches used to summon the wind with whistles made from alder, and fashioned pan pipes from the wood. If an invalid sits against an alder trunk, it is possible for a perceptive Witch to divine the nature of the illness by listening to the message whispered on the branches of the tree.

Almond

Scientific Name: *Prunus mygdalus communis*

Deities: the Sun God; the supreme creator god

Uses: The flower from the sweet almond (*var. dulcis*) makes a fine cosmetic emollient. Ground almond meal is an excellent facial scrub. Almond oil is used in furniture polish and in cooking (it lends the distinctive flavor to Mexican hot chocolate), but the prussic acid first must be removed. Eating almonds supposedly cures hangovers.

Magical Lore: Use almond wands for General Magic. The Hebrews fashion their seven-candle menorah from almond wood. Burn almond chips to improve business; carry the leaves in a pouch to gain wisdom. As the Greek legend goes, the gods changed Phyllis into the beautiful almond tree as recompense for her lover's desertion. When at last he returned and saw the leafless, forlorn tree, he clasped it to his bosom, and it burst into flower. Thus, the almond is commemorated as a symbol of love that persists even unto death.

> "Like to an Almond tree ymounted hige,
> On top of greene Selinis all alone, With blossoms brave bedecked daintly;
> Whose tender locks do tremble every one
> At everie little breath that under Heaven is blowne."
>
> Spenser, *The Fairy Queen*

Apple

Scientific Name: genus *Malus*

Deity: Aphrodite

Uses: Apples aid the digestion; so are served traditionally with fatty meats like goose and pork. They are said to help one retain youthful looks. Many kinds of apples exist including crab, cider, eaters, cookers. The fruitwood makes sturdy furniture and is used for mathematical drawing boards.

Magical Lore: Use the wood in Abra-Melin incense. Carve applewood to make wands for General Magic and Fertility Magic. The Druids beheld in the fruit a symbol of immortality, wisdom, and poetry. Therefore, they named their sacred island (probably modern-day Glastonbury) Avallon, the "Isle of the Apple Trees." In mythology, Iduna is reputed to have sent the gods a box of apples each day so that by their grace, she would always remain young. By tradition, women who want to conceive clasp their arms around an apple tree. To eat an apple at midnight on Hallowmas before a candlelit mirror is said to conjure one's Higher Genius. The apple was one of the sacred trees in the ancient Irish grove. Add red apple blossoms to springtime love spells and carry crushed apple leaves in a pouch to gain wisdom.

Ash

Scientific Name: genus *Fraxinus*

Common Names: Weeping Ash; White Ash (*F. americana*); Manna Ash (*F. ornus*).

Deities: Odin; Gwydion; Poseidon.

Uses: Ash is a tough, elastic timber used to hew spears, bows, and oars. Do not plant ash trees near other trees as they strangle the others' roots—from personal experience I can tell you that they send up suckers everywhere. The bark is tonic and astringent, and soothes skin diseases. Brew a tea from the bark and leaves to cure obesity, jaundice, arthritis, and snake bite.

Magical Lore: Make ash wands for Solar Magic or General Magic. Druidic ash wands were carved with spiral decorations, symbolic of rebirth. The Yggdrasill tree on which Odin hung himself to gain the secrets of the runes was an ash. Witches used to cut besoms from ash poles, birch twigs, and willow, and ride them to the Sabbats. Carry ash leaves for protection from drowning. Burn the leaves at Christmas in the Yule fire to dissolve crossed conditions and bring prosperity and unity to the family. The runic riddle about the ash states: "The aesc (ash), precious to men, is very tall. Firm on its base, it keeps its place securely, though many men attack it."

Aspen
Scientific Name: genus *Populus*
Common Name: Poplar (east of the Mississippi River)
Deities: the White Goddess; Saturn.
Uses: Since the wood provided shields for early peoples, this tree has always been associated with protection. The timber makes superior matches, match boxes, and paper pulp. The bark is a febrifuge, diuretic, and tonic, and helps conquer debility, gonorrhea, and gleet. The buds, when soaked with honey and distilled in water are said to improve vision.
Magical Lore: Since it falls under the jurisdiction of Saturn, the aspen is symbolic of old age and resurrection. Its day is the Fall Equinox, where in this part of the world, its golden colors are at their most resplendent. Jewelry fashioned from gilded aspen leaves reputedly bestow on the wearer a long and healthy life. Poplar buds, also called balm of gilead, are ingredients of Witches Flying Ointment and Nuit incense.

Barberry
Scientific Name: *Berberis vulgaris*
Common Names: Berberry; Pipperidge Bush
Deity: Mars
Uses: A yellow dye is rendered from the roots and ash of this spiny, yellow flowered shrub that colors the hair yellow. Barberry is an antiseptic, purgative,

and bitter stomachic tonic. It also makes a fine gargle for sore throat and a cure for the flu and ringworm. Eat the fruit as a garnish.

Magical Lore: Barberry formerly was called "Holy Thorn" because it was said to have formed part of Jesus' crown.

Beech

Scientific Name: genera *Fagus* and *Nothofagus*

Common Names: European Beech (*Fagus sylvatica*); American Beech (*F. grandifolia*)

Deities: Saturn

Uses: The wood is used to build parquet flooring, school desks, work benches, and bentwood furniture, and is a high quality heating fuel. The ash from the tree, rich in potash, provides a rich fertilizer. The beech is not a fussy tree; it can grow well in chalky, sandy soil. The leaves boiled in water cool and bind swelling, and can be drunk in a tea as an expectorant.

Magical Lore: Because the ancient Northmen carved runic tablets from beechwood, the name in Old German means "book." The Franks considered the beech an oracle tree and listened for messages whistled on the wind through its leaves.

Birch

Scientific Name: genus *Betula*

Common Names: Lady of the Wood, White Birch (*B. alba*), Silver Birch (*B. pendula*), Yellow Birch (*B. alleghaniensis*), River Birch (*B. nigra*), Paper Birch (*B. papyrifera*).

Deity: the Sun God

Uses: The oil softens leather and lends its scent to Russian leather perfume. The wood is useful for furniture-making and canoes, and the oil from the inner bark makes an excellent astringent, antiseptic, and relief for sore muscles.

Employ the leaves as an insect repellant. A decoction of the leaves acts as a sedative and laxative. Birch is also an old remedy for dropsy, gout, and kidney stones.

Magical Lore: The name is derived from a Sanscrit word that signifies "a tree whose bark is used for writing upon." By tradition, this tree represents inception, since it is the first to send forth leaves in the spring. If a maiden gives a piece of bark to a lover, it is a sign of encouragement. In the old days, delinquents and lunatics suffered flogging by birch whips because the tree was believed to drive out evil spirits from the body. Witches constructed their besoms from birch twigs for the same reason. The birch was a member of the ancient Irish sacred grove, and also was revered by Pagans throughout Scandinavia.

Blackthorn

Scientific Names: *Prunus domestica; Prunus spinosa.*
Common Names: Mother of the Wood; Sloe
Deities: Saturn; Hecate
Magical Lore: Include pieces from this thorny, white-flowered shrub in cursing spells and Black Magic. Use the thorns to pierce waxen images and Voodoo dolls. A curse invoked with a blackthorn wand is reputed to bring blight, poverty, and miscarriage upon the victim of the spell. The dark side of Odin's character is revealed by the fact that he carries a blackthorn staff.

Cedar

Scientific Names: genus *Cedrus;* genus *Thuja*
Common Names: Cedar of Lebanon (*Cedrus libani*); Eastern Red Cedar (*Juniperus virginiana*); Northern White Cedar (*Thuja occidentalis*); Tree of Life
Deities: Astarte; Jupiter

Uses: Aromatic cedarwood freshens closets and keeps out the moths. The wood also makes coffins and storage chests, totem poles, and dug-out canoes. Cedar is an astringent. It stimulates the heart muscle and helps cure coughs and scurvy. Thuja oil removes warts.

Magical Lore: Fumigate the temple with cedar incense. In ancient times, cedar was burned at sacrifices. The tree is a symbol of longevity, and some of the trees live for 2,000 years. Burn the wood to attract prosperity.

Cherry

Scientific Name: P*runus avium; P. podus;* and allies

Common Names: Black Cherry (*Prunus serotina*); Choke Cherry (*Prunus virginiana);* Bird Cherry (*P. padus*)

Deity: Aphrodite

Uses: Cherry provides an admirable cordial and syrup for coughs, colds, whooping cough, consumption, and sore throat. The wood is highly prized in furniture-making and wood sculpture. The inner bark relieves pain during childbirth and helps reduce *post partum* hemorrhage. An infusion of the bark conditions hair. The fruit is reputed to improve one's eyesight. When taken internally, the berries cause urine to flow. Cherry is also an astringent.

Magical Lore: Cherry is one of the magical needfire woods. Renew your supply each year, as the twigs spoil easily. The oil is the signature scent of Ritual perfume and is also used in Heart's Desire perfume.

Chestnut

Scientific Name: genus *Castanea*

Common Names: Sweet Chestnut

Deity: Jupiter

Uses: Although a poor fuel tree, the nuts furnish a nourishing repast, especially when used to stuff a turkey or a goose. Chestnut meal whitens cloth and makes a starch. Traditionally, the nuts powdered with honey and ingested were said to cure fever, ague, and blood-spitting.

Magical Lore: Add powdered chestnuts and leaves to the Winter Solstice Needfire mix.

Cypress

Scientific Name: *Cupressus cyparis* and genus *Chamaecyparis*
Common Names: Italian Cypress (*C. sempervivens*); Lawson Cypress (*Chamaecyparis lawsoniana*); Californian Monterey Cypress (*C. macrocarpa*); Atlantic White Cedar (*Chamaecyparis thyoides*)
Deities: Artemis; Saturn
Uses: A perennial evergreen that grows in a pyramidal shape and can live for 500 years. The dried cones are a binding agent that stops diarrhea, dysentery, excessive bleeding with menses, blood-spitting, and gum bleeding.
Magical Lore: Probably because of its longevity, cypress symbolizes death, funerals, and resurrection. Gazing at the tree was believed to mitigate sorrow for the loss of a loved one. Perhaps this is why it is a favorite graveyard tree. Burn cypress wood to consecrate your sword, and for past life workings.

Dogwood

Scientific Name: genus *Cornus*
Common Names: Cornelian Cherry (*C. mas*); Flowering Dogwood (*C. florida*)
Deities: Circe; Bran; Saturn
Uses: Pieces of dogwood bark distilled and dropped in water stupefy fish so they can be caught easily. This phenomenon is due to the bark's narcotic qualities. The bark also helps ameliorate toothache, fevers, neuralgia, and whooping cough. It is an antispasmodic for asthma, and taken as a tea, promotes sleep, although it is toxic in large doses. The fruit of the cornelian

cherry make a distinctive jam.

Magical Lore: Dogwood is the Mediterranean substitute for alder. Roman legend has it that Romulus threw a dogwood javelin into the air to decide the site for the city of Rome.

Elder

Scientific Name: genus *Sambucus*

Common Names: Black Elder (*S. nigra*); Red-Berried Elder (*S. racemosa*); Elderberry; Pipe Tree

Deity: Venus

Uses: The deep purple berries of the elder ripen in September, yet stay on the tree until late into December. Elderberry wine relieves headaches and the pain of ulcers. The berries also make tasty pies and preserves. Use the distilled flowers as an eyewash or as a cleanser to remove dead skin cells from your face. A black dye is extracted from the berries, and the leaves are a diaphoretic when drunk as a tea, and the inner bark is a cathartic. The ancient Greeks and Romans fabricated musical instruments from the wood.

Magical Lore: Use elder wands for spirit exorcisms. By tradition, cradles should not be built from elder wood, because it is said that this will infuriate the Elder Mother, the spirit of the tree, and she will push and pinch the child in the cradle until it is removed. Supposedly, Irish Witches rode to Sabbats on elder besoms. An English superstition associates elder (like cypress) with funerals, and claims that the elder brings the devil into the house. Thus, elder is considered an unlucky wood in needfire mix. According to one superstition, it is considered a tree of doom. However, elder grown in the shape of a cross that flowers on the grave is said to indicate that the spirit of the deceased is at peace. Judas supposedly hung himself on an elder, so the tree has become a symbol of grief to Christians. If you cut round discs from elder pith and soak them in oil and float them on water on Christmas Eve, it is said that a vision will appear to you to let you know who else in the neighborhood is a Witch.

Elm

Scientific Name: genus *Ulmus*
Common Names: American Elm *(U. americana)*; English Elm; *(U. procera)*
Slippery Elm; *(U. fulva);* Rock Elm *(U. thomasii)*
Deities: Bacchus; Dionysus
Uses: Elms provide sturdy chair seats, coffins, and packing cases. The bruised leaves mixed with vinegar make a cosmetic wash. As a poultice, the leaves alleviate the symptoms of gout. Steeped in vinegar, they make a stimulating facial. A decoction of the bark cures ringworm and skin diseases.
Magical Lore: The elm was revered because it supported the grape vine, which was sacred to the wine god. In my opinion, the problem with the elm, is that it is a tree inimical to humanity. Favored by city planners, elms grew to stately heights in cities and suburbs in this country, when suddenly they were attacked by Dutch elm disease, a devastating illness that strikes down hundreds of thousands of trees. I remember growing up in suburban Detroit where the elms were attacked, and how unfortunate the neighborhood looked after the disease had run its course. Elms also have the habit of suddenly dropping branches on unsuspecting passersby, and their seeds leave an untidy mess on lawns and clog sewers. Elms have a low resistance to urban pollution. Perhaps the tree is paying us back for its inability to survive in an urban environment we have inflicted on it.

Fir

Scientific Names: genera *Abies* and *Pseudotsuga* (Douglas Fir)
Common Names: European Silver Fir *(A. alba)*; Balsam Fir *(A. balsamea)*;
Noble Fir *(A.procera)*
Deities: Artemis; Athene; Jupiter
Uses: The wood is serviceable in building. Turpentine which is extracted from the pitch, cleanses ulcers and wounds. The needles are known as a cure for gonorrhea and lung infections. Silver fir also contains diuretic properties.

Magical Lore: Silver fir holds the place of honor in the tree calendar as the first day of the year. The tree is sacred to the goddesses, Artemis and Selene, who preside over childbirth. Candles made from fir and burned at the bedside of a new mother and child protect them from evil-wishers.

Gorse

Scientific Name: *Ulex europeus*
Common Names: Furze; Broom; Golden Gorse; Whin
Deities: Bran; Mars; Morwyn
Uses: This low, prickly shrub that grows in wastelands, along cliffsides, and in gravelly areas as tall as four to five feet, is covered with cheerful, yellow flowers almost year-long. Farmers burn off the old thorny parts in the spring so that the animals can reach the tender green shoots. The flowers cure jaundice, scarlet fever, and snakebite.
Magical Lore: Also known as Onn, the gorse is the tree of the Spring Equinox, and should be added to the spring and summer needfires. Because it flowers bright yellow and is burned in the spring to create fodder, it is associated with the springtime god and goddess, and is considered a fire tree. It is reputed to ward off black magic spells. I have seen gorse growing in dazzling profusion on the Isle of Caldey off the southern coast of Wales. A group of Cistercian monks, who have built a monastery there and taken a vow of silence, concoct an exquisite perfume from the flowers. If you ever get an opportunity to acquire this rare perfume, you will not be disappointed by its seductive scent.

Hawthorn

Scientific Name: genus *Crataegus*
Common Names: Haw; May Tree; Cheese Tree; Ladies' Meet; Hagthorn; Cockspur (*C. crus-galli*)
Deities: Blodenwedd; Olwen; Flora; Cardea

Uses: This thorny tree bears white flowers that so smell of decay, that bees are repelled by the odor. The flowers are pollinated solely by flies. The hard wood, in some respects, burns better than oak. Because they are bushy trees, they provide living fences on farmland. The wine of the hawthorn berry alleviates internal pains and reputedly draws out thorns. The berries soothe a sore throat when taken in a decoction, are a cardiac, diuretic, astringent, and tonic.

Magical Lore: Carve hawthorn wands for White Magic, protection, and power spells. It is said that the hedge that grew overnight in the Sleeping Beauty legend was a hawthorn. For a long time, English peasants believed that hawthorn flowers still carried the smell of the London plague. Country folk would tie strips of clothing to the hawthorn trees that flourished around sacred wells to mourn the dead. Originally, Cardea, a hag aspect of the goddess, who is said to have abhorred marriage, often worked spells with a hawthorn wand against those who married at this unlucky time of year. Thus, the hawthorn month in the tree calender (see chapter 6) was viewed as the month of enforced chastity. People were supposed not to change their old clothes until the month was over, and only after they had cleaned the entire house in their old clothes were they allowed to throw them away. Later, the month came to be associated with voluptuousness and fertility, and as such, fell under the jurisdiction of the love goddess, Flora. Young people trekked to the forest on the first of May and gathered garlands of blossoms to decorate the maypole. This change in association for the hawthorn tree has made it the marriage tree. Now it is used in spells of love and union.

Hazel

Scientific Name: genus *Corylus*
Deities: Mercury; the Muses; the Caryatid (nut fairies)
Uses: Hazel nuts ground with mead are an old remedy for coughs. Hazel liqueur is delicious, and appropriate to imbibe on the Sabbats. Some varieties yield nuts superbly suited to dessert-making.
Magical Lore: Hazel wood furnishes the best wands for General Magic,

Healing Magic, and Communication Magic (telepathy, etc.). The hazel nut represents concentrated wisdom. In Tipperary, at a sacred spot called Connla's Well, hazel nuts dropped into the mouths of ancient salmon supposedly made them wise. From this legend the hazel earned its reputation as the tree of poetic inspiration. King MacCuill of Ireland, was named the "son of the hazel." Forked hazel twigs supposedly find water and buried treasures by a process called dowsing, and ferret out thieves and murderers. An old custom has it that maidens who give hazel twigs to their would-be suitors are advising them in a subtle way to abandon their pursuits.

Holly

Scientific Name: genus *Ilex*

Common Names: Christ's Thorn; Oak Holly (*Quercus ilex*); Native American Holly (*I. apoca*). European Holly (*I. aquifolium*); and Scarlet Oak (*Q. coccinea*) were probably the original hollies referred to by the Celtic people in their tree calendar, as these were trees indigenous to Britain.

Deities: Mars; the fairy spirits

Uses: Holly is a diaphoretic. The decoction of the leaves works successfully in cases of catarrh, pleurisy, and smallpox. The berries are a violent emetic and purgative, as well as an astringent. A decoction of the berries will check bleeding, although the berries themselves should be avoided because they are poisonous.

Magical Lore: As the oak tree rules the waxing year, so the holly, oak holly, or scarlet oak rules the waning year. Holly (the word means "holy") is a favorite Christmas plant. The bright red berries remind Christians of Christ's Passion. The custom of decorating with shiny, dark green holly branches harkens back to the Romans who, during the Saturnalia, decked their homes with these and other evergreen branches, and the Druids also festooned their huts with holly branches in winter to provide a dwelling place for sylvan spirits. Custom dictates that to plant holly near a house defends it from poison and lightning. Also it is believed that if one throws the wood at a rampant animal, it immediately will back off and lie down. However, I wouldn't count on it! Holly flowers cast into water are said to freeze it. In the *Romance of*

Gawain and the Green Knight, the Green Knight, who spares Gawain, carries a club made from holly wood. Holly is one of the sacred Irish trees along with apple, ash, birch, hazel, oak, and willow.

Ivy

Scientific Name: *Hedera helix*
Common Name: English Ivy
Deities: Bacchus; Dionysus; Osiris; Saturn
Uses: Culpeper writes that the yellow berries cure jaundice, express urine, induce menses, dissolve kidney stones, and prevent plague! Boil the leaves in vinegar and apply externally for sideaches, and to the temples for headaches. Ivy boiled in butter and applied to the skin lessens sunburn pain.
Magical Lore: Ivy is thought to be a resurrection plant, perhaps because it grows in a spiral form. The leaves formed the poets' crown and the wreath for Bacchus. As a symbol of the inspiration of Bacchus, ivy-and-silver-fir ale was served up during the Bacchanals. Also, because porous ivy wood was used to separate wine from water, tavern signs were often painted to show sprigs of ivy.

Juniper

Scientific Names: genus *Juniperus* and *J. communis*
Uses: The mature (at least two-year-old) berries of this shrubby tree contain stomachic, emmenagogue, carminative, fungicidal, and diuretic properties. They also flavor gin.
 Juniper is hailed as a cure for a variety of ailments, including flatulence, venereal disease, indigestion, and kidney and bladder infections. The leaves brewed into a tea ameliorate the pains of childbirth. In a decoction, they also are applied by veterinarians to exposed wounds on animals, and as a fly deterrent. The dry, resinous foliage is used to smoke ham and cheese.
Magical Lore: Burn juniper berries when performing American Indian Shamanic Magic to protect the Circle from negativity.

Laurel

Scientific Name: *Laurus nobilis*

Common Names: Bay Tree; Daphne; Sweet Bay

Deity: Apollo

Uses: This native of Southern Europe can be grown in tubs and shaped into rounded balls. It is a diaphoretic, emetic, and excitant. The leaves sprinkled in the bath alleviate menstrual cramps and pain from bladder infections, and help mend skin irritations, including cuts and bruises. If ground into a paste, the leaves make a stimulating facial mask. The oil and berries provoke delayed menses, induce birthing, and help expel afterbirth. Too strong a dose at the wrong time may cause miscarriage. The leaves are employed in cooking, especially to flavor Portuguese sardines. Use in solar incenses.

Magical Lore: Laurel, especially when hung over a doorway, is credited with dispelling the negative effects of Saturn and drives away the effects of Black Magic, poltergeists, and general negativity. The priestesses at Delphi relied on the leaves as oracles, and it is said that a leaf added to the first cup of tea in the morning improves the memory. Laurel leaves are burned in incense to conjure spirits and procure love. Writers have been known to pass a bay leaf over a sheet of blank paper to entice the Muses to lend their inspiration. To make wishes come true, gather seventy laurel leaves on a Sunday and attach them to seventy sheets of parchment paper. Drop them into a moving body of water, and pray to Apollo to grant your wish. What you desire should come to pass within seven days, seven weeks, or seven months. To cause a woman to love you forever, secrete three leaves at the foot of her bed. To secure a husband, write the name of the one you desire with dove's blood ink three times on three leaves (nine times total). Soak the leaves for twenty-four hours in olive oil to which you have added several drops of Heart's Desire anointing oil. Remove the leaves and wrap them in a red cord. Enclose them in a mojo bag, and wear the bag or carry it in your purse or pocket. Perform this spell at dawn on a Friday.

Maple

Scientific Name: genus *Acer*

Common Names: Silver Maple (*A. saccharorum*); Sugar Maple (*A. saccharum*); Sycamore (*A. pseudoplatinus* - Great Britain only); Norway Maple (*A. platanoides*); Field Maple (*A. campestre*)

Deity: Jupiter

Uses: As far as I know, the maple has no traditional magical uses and is not considered a magical tree, but it should be. Its great beauty at any time of the year, but particularly in the fall when the leaves display brilliant colors, is a joy to all. The wood of this stately tree is highly prized in furniture-making, and it supplies fuel wood and charcoal. The sap of the maple tree, when made into sugar candies or maple syrup, delights children of all ages. In addition, the bark is an astringent, and a decoction of the leaves alleviates sore and bloodshot eyes. For all the service the maple provides, I think it should be better recognized. If you know of a maple or a grove of maples in your area, I urge you to meditate before these trees and communicate with their spirits. Record the impressions you receive so you that can later devise spells centered around this special tree.

Mistletoe

Scientific Name: *Viscum album*

Common Names: All-Heal; American Mistletoe (*V. flavescen*); (*V. album*). (The first two stimulate the circulatory system and muscles of the uterus and raise blood pressure, while the English species, *V. album,* does just the reverse

Deities: the Sun God; Jupiter

Uses: Mistletoe is a parasite that grows in the branches of other trees. It is considered poisonous, but has been employed with care successfully as a narcotic, antispasmotic, emetic, nervine, and aphrodisiac. Supposedly it helps to cure ulcers, stop convulsions, and ripen tumors and swellings. The Druids believed it cured sterility. However, since it is poisonous, I do not recommend using it.

Magical Lore: When the Druids received a certain vision, they gathered in white robes and went in search of a mistletoe that grew on an oak (a rare occurrence). They would spread a net below the tree, climb it, and cut the mistletoe with a golden sickle, taking care that none dropped on the ground; for to allow this to happen would bring ruin to all. Because of the Druidic belief in its fertilizing powers, mistletoe is still the plant that lovers kiss beneath at Christmas. In another story about the mistletoe, it once was considered an unfortunate plant because it killed the Norse god, Balder. However, the gods so loved Balder that they overruled the mistletoe's destructive power and resurrected their beloved kin. They declared that henceforth, the mistletoe would be the emblem of eternal love. To draw a lover, burn dried leaves, berries, and twigs. Wrap the ashes in a paper, tie the bundle around your neck, and wear it for thirty days. The Australian aborigines hold that mistletoe harbors the souls of spirits awaiting rebirth. To find the solution to your problems, decorate your altar with mistletoe and light a white candle. Meditate on your difficulties for twenty minutes each night. You soon will find the answer.

Myrtle

Scientific Name: *Myrtus communis*
Common Name: Bayberry Bark; Waxberry; Wax Myrtle
Deities: Aphrodite; Moon; Mercury
Uses: The fragrant berries of this little tree deter diarrhea, dysentery, and breast cancer. A decoction of the mildly astringent leaves makes a vaginal douche. Add the leaves to facial sauna steam herbs and Libra incense.
Magical Lore: Because the leaves of the myrtle are forever green, it is considered a resurrection tree, and a Christian symbol of compassion. The plant, sacred to Aphrodite, is an ingredient in love potions, incenses, and spells. It is believed to be a lucky plant, and is included in herbal talismans for prosperity and good fortune. Myrtle oil is supposed to bring the wearer a large family, long life, youthful appearance, and good health. To dream of myrtle presages wealth or a legacy.

Oak

Scientific Name: genus *Quercus*
Common Names: Tanner's Bark; (*Q. robur*); White Oak (*Q. alba*); Northern Red Oak; (*Q. borealis*)
Deities: Zeus; Jupiter; Llyr; the Dagda; Janus; and all thunder gods
Uses: Acorns render a delicious bread, rich in protein, and were a staple food

among the ancient Celtic and Germanic tribes. The wood is both hard and tough, the best for shipbuilding, furniture, and firewood. King Arthur's Round Table, constructed from a single slice of a gigantic oak, is still on display in England. Oak bark is rich in tannin, which is ideal for treating hides and leather. A decoction of the bark alleviates vomiting and blood-spitting. Oak buds distilled in water quell fevers and dissolve kidney stones. The strongly antiseptic and astringent leaves, are employed in remedies against ague, hemorrhage, chronic dysentery, piles, and bleeding gums.

Magical Lore: This is the supreme Druid's tree, perfect for carving oak wands for Druidic and General Magic. Traditionally, the needfire was kindled inside an oak log. Shape your Pentacle and magic mirror frame from the wood. The acorn is a symbol of male fertility and power, as it resembles the male sex organ. To predict whether the spring will be wet, the old English rhyme goes:

> *If the oak's before the ash*
> *Then you'll only get a splash;*
> *If the ash precedes the oak,*
> *Then you may expect a soak.*[31]

It is believed that oaks draw lightning, and that fairies will enter a house built of oak logs through the knotholes. Herne the Hunter is thought to haunt the oaks of Windsor Forest, and stories of other haunted oaks survive throughout England. The French used to build chapels of oak, and holy oaks still exist in Lower Saxony and Westphalia. The nuns of St. Brigit at Kildere maintain a "shrine of the oak" with a perpetual fire, a tradition rooted in the times of the worship of the fire goddess. Oak galls, which are round speckled eggs made from insect larvae that inhabit the oak, were called serpent eggs by the Druids, and were worked into love charms. These "eggs" can also be powdered and used as a douche, gargle, and cure against dysentery. Since the oak rules the first half of the Druidic year, it is symbolic of a door, swinging on its hinges, welcoming in the season. Therefore, the tree is associated with Janus and all portal deities.

Olive

Scientific Name: *Olea europaea*

Deities: Athena; Minerva; Apollo

Uses: The oil from this tree that can live for 2,000 years is used in cooking and as an emollient in soaps and massage oil. It is also a laxative. The leaves are astringent and antiseptic, and effective against insect bites, dandruff, inflammations, and fevers. The olive is a Mediterranean tree, although it is also grown commercially in California, and a few are known to survive in Cornwall.

Magical Lore: The olive branch, a symbol of peace, is proffered in the mouth of a dove. A branch was always presented to the victor of the ancient Greek Olympic games. The olive tree was so important to the Greeks that those who cultivated it were exempt from military service. The olive is important to the Judeo-Christian tradition as well, and is mentioned in the Bible more frequently than any other tree. Many cultures burned olive oil in temple lamps to symbolize purity and fruitfulness.

Pine

Scientific Name: genus *Pinus*

Common Names: Scots Pine *(P. sylvestris);* Jersey Pine *(P. virginiana)*; Ponderosa *(P. ponderosa)*; White Pine *(P. strobus)*

Deities: Pan, Cernunnos, and all forest gods.

Uses: Pine trees have a high commercial value as timber; the resin is used as violin rosin and in incense-making. Veterinarians prepare medications from parts of the tree that are antiseptic, stimulant, diuretic, and diaphoretic. Pine needles are a rubefacient, and when used as an inhalant, are a stimulant to the mucous membranes and respiratory system. Pine oil creates an invigorating bath. Also it is an ingredient of liniments and plasters.

Magical Lore: Pine is one of the seven Irish chieftain trees. Burn it in needfire mix and in shamanistic incenses.

Pomegranate

Scientific Name: *Punica granatum*

Deities: Persephone; Adonis

Uses: The fruit of this scrubby tree is about the size and shape of an orange, but has a much harder peel. The seeds are a demulcent; the rind stops diarrhea; the fruit is a mild astringent and fever refrigerant; the tannicide bark causes vomiting. The pulp of the fruit can be dried, powdered, and used to fasten teeth.

Magical Lore: Pomegranate is regarded a symbol of fertility because of its many seeds. The fruit is eaten in Circle at the Winter Solstice, and as a part of fertility spells. Because Persephone tasted the pomegranate fruit, she was consigned to remain in the Underworld during the dark half of the year.

Reed

Scientific Name: genus *Phragmites*

Deity: Osiris

Uses: The Irish used to thatch their roofs with reeds, which reinforced the idea of the tree as a symbol of established power. It is the material from which royal scepters and arrow shafts are made.

Magical Lore: Use reed wands in Egyptian Magic as staffs, or as scepters of office. Since the reed has a natural hollow in the shaft, it is easy to use it as a wand and insert metal rods or tinctures for magical purposes. Our coven possesses a reed wand of office that exchanges hands with whoever leads the coven for a six months' term. This is the twelfth tree in the tree calendar, and since the number stands for established power, the reed makes an appropriate symbol of office.

Rowan

Scientific Name: *Sorbus aucuparia; S. americana*
Common Names: Mountain Ash; Quickbeam. "Rowan" originates from the Gaelic word, *ruadh-an* ("red ones").
Deities: Brigit, the Muses; Cuchulain
Uses: One source states that the seeds are dangerous because they contain cyanide, but the bark can be decocted and used to cure diarrhea. Others maintain that birds love the berries, and that although they are too sour for humans, they make tasty preserves. Mrs. Grieve tells us that the Welsh used to brew an ale from the berries, but that the recipe is now lost.[32]
Magical Lore: The rowan is considered the quickening tree and the knowledge tree, and the wine is said to endow one with poetic inspiration. Cut rowan wands for protection and divination. The twigs are used as dowsing rods to find buried metals. By tradition, the rowan is an oracular tree like the beech and the oak, that solves riddles. Celts were said to immobilize bewitched horses or ghosts with rowan stakes. The berries were called the "food of the gods," which is one way of saying that it was taboo for humans. A cross made of rowan twigs and tied with red thread is a charm against Witchcraft and lightning. Go to a rowan tree when your strength is depleted, and be revived.

Vine

Scientific Name: *Vitis vinifera*
Common Names: Grape Vine
Deities: Bacchus; Dionysus; Osiris; solar deities
Uses: The dried fruit (raisins, currants) alleviates coughs and consumption and is mildly laxative. Vine ash is said to whiten the teeth. Grape sugar differs from other sugars in that it enters the circulation without any salivary action. Sometimes it is ingested by triathletes who need to boost their blood sugar levels. Boiled leaves combined with a lotion, or made into a poultice alleviate external inflammation and irritations. The leaves are reputed to stop hemorrhages.

Magical Lore: The bramble was substituted for the vine in Great Britain, because the vine does not grow well there. The vine is sacred to the wine god, and the month in the tree calendar represents the vintage season. It is said that it is a month of joy and exhilaration, but also the month of wrath. The vine symbolizes the exalted poet.

Walnut

Scientific Name: genus *Julgans*
Common Names: American Black Walnut *(J. nigra)*
Deities: Jupiter; the Sun God
Uses: Walnut is a favorite tree of squirrels. The nuts, so difficult to separate from the hard shell, are this rodent's epicurean delight. The kernels steeped in red wine supposedly keep hair from falling out. The leaf juice will dye skin brown. Walnut is an astringent, detergent, and laxative. A decoction of the leaves ameliorates eczema, and the kernels cure wounds, carbuncles, and gangrene.

Whitten

Scientific Name: *Sambucus ebubus*
Common Names: Dwarf Elder; The Wayfaring Tree; Water Elder; Danewort
Deity: Aphrodite
Uses: This low shrub displays pretty white flowers etched in purple or black. The flowers remedy gout, piles, women's diseases, and eye inflammations. The bark and seeds cure jaundice, and the buds are said to relax the bowels. The leaves can be distilled in oil to alleviate boils and painful joints. The leaves also drive mice from the barn. American Dwarf Elder (*Aralia hispida*) grows to the height of only one to two feet, and the flowers have a fetid odor. However, the bark of this shrub is used as a diuretic and a cure for dropsy.
Magical Lore: The whitten was thought to have sprung from the blood of slain Danes.

Willow

Scientific Name: genus *Salix*

Common Names: White Willow (*S. alba*); Osier (any willow); Weeping Willow (*S. babylonica*).

Deities: Circe; Hecate; Hera; Ceridwen; Persephone; the Moon Goddess.

Uses: The bark and seeds of the white willow stop blood- spitting, bleeding from the womb, and vomiting. The bark and leaves soaked in wine help remove dandruff. The bark contains salicylic acid, which is related to aspirin. Mix it with borax and patchouli and apply as a deodorant.

Magical Lore: At one time willow was thought to cure rheumatism, because folks thought that this disease was generated by Witchcraft. Fashion willow wands to work Moon Magic and enchantments. The willow is thought of as a sea tree, and is associated with all bodies of water.

Witch Hazel

Scientific Name: *Hamamelis virginiana*

Deities: the Moon Goddess; Diana

Uses: The astringent rendered by Witch Hazel bark has been marketed for years by the Dickinson company to relieve pain and itching from insect bites, rashes, and burning feet. Witch hazel tea reputedly stops stomach bleeding, bowel complaints, and excessive bleeding at menses. When used as a poultice, it is supposed to break up cellulite.

Magical Lore: Witch hazel wands are used to divine the location of underground water; hence, its name.

Yew

Scientific Name: genus *Taxus*

Deities: Hecate; Saturn

Uses: One yew at Tandridge Church, Surrey, England, that measures forty-five feet in diameter is estimated to be 2,500 years old. Yew provides superior firewood, fence posts, wood for long bows, and decorative furniture. All parts of the tree are extremely poisonous. Cases of cattle poisoning have occurred where the cattle were allowed to graze in churchyards where yews were planted.

Magical Lore: In Ireland, wine barrels constructed of yew were called "the coffins of the vine." The Irish also used yew wands in Magic, and lighted the needfire in a hollowed-out yew log instead of in an oak. Since yew trees are planted in churchyards, a superstition developed in Brittany that claimed that a root from the yew could spread to the mouths of each corpse buried there. The custom of planting yews in churchyards probably originates with the Druids, who built their shrines in yew groves.

Notes

1. *Man, Myth, and Magic,* vol. 17, London, Parnell, 1970, p. 480.

2. Israel Regardie, *The Golden Dawn,* vol. 3, St. Paul, Llewellyn Publications, 1978, p. 14.

3. *The Golden Dawn,* p. 10.

4. Cyril Scott, *Music: Its Secret Influence Throughout the Ages,* Wellingborough, England, The Aquarian Press, 1982 (rpt 1933).

5. Joseph Frank, *The Widening Gyre: Crisis and Mastery in Modern Literature,* Bloomington, Indiana, University of Indiana Press, 1968 (rpt 1963), p. 81.

6. *The Widening Gyre,* p. 175.

7. Roderyk Lange, *The Nature of Dance: An Anthropological Perspective,* New York, International Publications Services, 1976, p. 61.

8. Kenneth Hurlstone Jackson, *A Celtic Miscellany,* New York, Penguin Classics, 1977 (rpt 1951), p. 86.

9. Morwyn, *Secrets of a Witch's Coven,* West Chester, Pennsylvania, Whitford Press, 1988, p. 197.

10. *Secrets of a Witch's Coven,* p. 196

11. *Isaiah,* I., 2.

12. J.E. Cirlot, *A Dictionary of Symbols,* translation, New York, Philosophical Library, Inc., 1983, p. 6.

13. Aleister Crowley, *Magick,* York Beach, Maine, Weiser, 1984 (rpt 1973), p. 115.

14. *A Celtic Miscellany,* Welsh englyn by Gwilym Cowlyd, 1827-1905, p. 126.

15. Ibid, John Ceiriog Hughes, p. 86.

16. Ibid, Irish, author unknown, eighth-ninth century, p. 128.

17. Barbara Lehman, "The Trolls," in Elizabeth Pepper and John Wilcox, *The Witches' Almanac,* Cambridge, Massachusetts, Pentangle Press, 1978, p. 20.

18. Charles Kinsley, *The Water Babies,* Garden City, New York, Dodd and Mead Co., Inc., 1937 (rpt 1911), pp. 58-59.

19. From the rock musical, *Hair.*

20. Patricia Crowther, *Lid Off the Cauldron: A Handbook for Witches,* London, Frederick Muller Ltd., p. 115.

21. Jean Auel, *The Clan of the Cave Bear,*. New York, Bantam, 1981 (rpt 1980).

22. Robert Graves, *The White Goddess,* New York, Farrar, Straus and Giroux, 1974 (rpt 1948), p. 398.

23. Recipe for "Picau Ar y Maen," Sian Llewellyn, *The Welsh Kitchen: Recipes from Wales,* Cardiff, 1972, p. 40.

24. I discuss how to perform the Middle Pillar Ritual in *Secrets of the Witch's Coven,* pp. 100-103.

25. Herman Slater, A Book of Pagan Rituals, vol I, New York, Earth Religions, 1974, p. 19.

26. Regardie, *The Golden Dawn ,* vol. 2, book 3, o. 3.

27. Slater, *A Book of Pagan Rituals,* p. 59

28. Translated by Morwyn from Niveo Ramos Sales, *Brazilian Recipes, Fascinations and Enchantments,* Rio de Janeiro, Achiami, 1982, p. 22.

29. Antonio Texeira Alves Neto, *A magia e os encantos da Pomba Gira,* Rio de Janeiro, Editora Eco, 1975, pp. 41-42, trans. by Morwyn.

30. Graves, *The White Goddess,* p. 209.

31. Doreen Valiente, *Natural Magic,* St. Martin's Press,1975, p. 134.

32. Mrs. Grieve, *A Modern Herbal,* vol I., England, Dover, 1971 (rpt 1931), p. 70.